D1569066

SUBMITTING TO FREEDOM

RELIGION IN AMERICA SERIES
Harry S. Stout
General Editor

SUBMITTING TO FREEDOM

The Religious Vision of William James

BENNETT RAMSEY

New York   Oxford
OXFORD UNIVERSITY PRESS
1993

Oxford University Press

Oxford New York Toronto
Delhi Bombay Calcutta Madras Karachi
Kuala Lumpur Singapore Hong Kong Tokyo
Nairobi Dar es Salaam Cape Town
Melbourne Auckland

and associated companies in
Berlin Ibadan

Copyright © 1993 by Bennett Ramsey

Published by Oxford University Press, Inc.,
200 Madison Avenue, New York, NY 10016

Library of Congress Cataloging-in-Publication Data
Ramsey, Bennett.
Submitting to freedom : the religious vision of William James / Bennett Ramsey.
p. cm. (Religion in America series) Includes bibliographical references and index.
ISBN 0-19-507426-2
1. James, William, 1842–1910—Contributions in religious thought.
I. Title. II. Series: Religion in America series (Oxford University Press)
B945.J24R36 1993 291'.092—dc20
92-5060

1 3 5 7 9 8 6 4 2

Printed in the United States of America
on acid-free paper

To Rebecca

ACKNOWLEDGMENTS

As this is a book about the relationships that obtain and are primary in our individual efforts, it is appropriate to preface what is about to be said by acknowledging at least some of those who influenced this book's writing. First and foremost, I would like to acknowledge Tom Driver, through whose wisdom this book gained whatever insight it might contain about the drama of human relations. Acknowledgment goes out as well to my initial set of readers, James Washington, Wayne Proudfoot, Cornel West, and Gerald Sheppard, who provided constructive, critical insight into William James and my attempts to understand him and, in the case of West, Washington, and Sheppard, dogged me about the book until I submitted and sent it out for publication. Sally MacNichol, Richard Werner, and John Sopper served as primary conversation partners during the period in which I revised my work. I thank them for their insights and endurance; their thoughts and concerns lie at the heart of my own thoughts about James. A special word of acknowledgment is owed to Henry Levinson, whose knowledge about James gave the critical stimulus to my thinking, and whose support for and affirmation of my redescription of James helped to bring this book to life. Finally, I am deeply thankful to Lisa Huestis, whose conviction and encouragement brought me across those gaps where the courage of my convictions failed.

April 1992   B. R.
Decatur, Georgia

Contents

SUBMITTING TO FREEDOM

Introduction

This book is about several things, and it seems a courtesy to the reader to explain, at least preliminarily, what they are. First and foremost, the book is about William James, or rather about his writings and his work. What I have attempted to do is present an overall description of the patterns in James's writings, the manner in which they developed, and the ends to which they led. My purpose is fairly straightforward. I want to provide the reader with a general guide to James's thought so that specific writings may be encountered with some sense of their place in the body of his work.

I also want to advance an argument about the nature of James's work overall: that it finds its whither and its whence in a developing understanding and an increasingly strong avowal of the human person as a religiously bounded self. I see James as absorbed, throughout most of his work, with the investigation and consideration of religious problems. More to the point, I see him attempting to broaden the definition of religion beyond the confines of theistic and supernaturalistic frameworks toward an immanentist, almost naturalistic meaning. Above all, I see James as advocating a religious way of life, a way of being based not on control but on respect for and responsibility to the immanent ties and powers that bind the self.

As such, this book tends toward being a rather old-fashioned intellectual history. I am after the central and continuous problematic at the heart of James's intellectual efforts. I want to offer alternatives both to those intellectual histories that argue that

James is a systematic philosopher with only a passing and sub-sidiary interest in religion, and to those studies that accept the fact of his religious concerns but limit his work in religion to philo-sophical arguments about the status of religious claims and the assertion of foundationalist notions about the autonomy and origi-nality of our experience of the divine.[1] Although my intention is not just to display the development of James's thought, this is certainly a central concern. In this regard I suggest that the usual scholarly division of James's writings into three parts (early philosophical and psychological works; a middle period of "tender-minded" reli-gious investigation; and a late, strictly philosophical period) is misleading: it serves the interests of antireligious scholars rather than the interests of William James, and it offers a view of James that disregards the broadening and deepening of his understanding of religion in his later works.

In addition to being a work of intellectual history, this book is also generalist in nature. That is, it takes as its task the generalist's project of, in Lewis Mumford's words, "bringing together widely separated fields . . . into a larger common area, visible only from the air."[2] To be sure, there is always some forfeiture of detail when work is general; that is the inevitable result of taking a bird's-eye view. The present state of James scholarship, however, is such that his writing has been too much dissected, divided up, and fenced in by detail workers and specialists. There is a need for a text in which James's thought is pieced back together, if only so that new details may become apparent.

There is also a need for a contextual study of James's thought. Simply put, too many writers have succumbed to the temptation just to pick up and stroll along with William James. A traditional scholarly bias toward positivistic approaches to texts, coupled with the plasticity of James's thought and the similarity of his concerns to our own, has too often led scholars simply to deal with what James said in his texts and to forget about further considerations.[3] To work in that way is to lose both the focus and the location of what James produced; it is also to ignore the social responsibility that he saw as integral to his efforts.[4] If the content of James's writings is to become clear, efforts must be made to elucidate not only his texts but also the context in which those texts were written.

Context, of course, is a slippery word, and can mean a variety of things. In the case of James, his texts could be set in an individual context, with biographical data as the key. Or his work could be investigated with an eye on his professional and academic context, in which case his intellectual heritage, his disputes with the idealists, positivists, and so on, would be central. Finally, James's writings could be seen within the framework of a private context, in reference to his letters, relationships, and personal crises. All of these methods have their uses, although, I believe, to only a limited extent.[5]

My own procedure in this book has been to evaluate James's texts within their cultural context. I have done this not out of personal preference but rather because that is what James's texts tell us to do. The majority of his writings were originally lectures and public addresses, essays directed at cultured but nonscholarly audiences, or textbooks designed for general use. In turn, those writings indicate that James may best be understood if we see him as an organic intellectual and representative thinker—as a popular writer, to put it in the pejorative phrase used by many of his critics—one working in and through a community with common cultural conceptions and understandings.

My treatment of James is thus in part as much about late nineteenth-century North American culture as it is about James himself. He is examined in the light of the group consciousness of his middle class and culture. His writings are investigated in terms of the cultural problems and conceptions he drew upon, sometimes accepted, and oftentimes tried to overcome. Each of the two major sections of this book begins with a cultural study that sets the stage for the investigation of James's work. I introduce his early writings through an analysis of the collapse of middle-class culture in the years following the Civil War. I start the examination of his later writings with a look at the attempted revival of that middle-class culture at the turn of the twentieth century.

Much of what is said in these two contextual chapters should be familiar to readers with a basic competence in American cultural history. I have attempted to use sources that are, for the most part, fairly accessible and well known. I have drawn upon the thought of scholars in the field of cultural history whose interpretations have received significant comment and appraisal. I work through these sources and interpretations, however, with a very particular aim, for I am interested in discussing not just the state of the culture—which norms were viable, which were not, and how they interplayed—but what was at stake when this or that set of cultural norms developed or died out.

Thus, in the initial chapter of the book I take as my subject matter what is usually referred to as the "spiritual crisis of the Gilded Age."[6] Here I try to show what that crisis was all about, and to delineate its various dimensions. In agreement with many others I say that America's cultural norms lost their force under the impact of the experience of the war, a conflict between religious and secular scientific paradigms, and an increasingly corporate, technocratic, and bureaucratic structuring of society. But I try to show, too, that the heart of the crisis was a perception of the contingency of the human person. Simply put, the breakdown of the standing cultural order exposed Americans to the recognition—overall a debilitating one—that they lived in a world without foundations.

The center of my argument in the chapter—and it is here that James enters directly—is that the cultural collapse of the post–Civil War era was a collapse fundamentally in definitions of the self: the separate, autonomous, and independent self of the Enlightenment, which had needed correspondences to an absolute realm in order to construct its transcendent life, lost those correspondences and any sense that they could be reattained. Intrinsic natures, an absolute realm, the "eternal verities"—all of these were seen through. To the extent that appeals to them continued to be made, they were understood to be but fictions of the real with no authoritative sway, platitudes and dead metaphors with little binding force.

As a result of this loss of absolutes, the self seemed on the verge of dissolving into purposelessness and the "I" of losing its determining power. People began to see themselves as only another part of nature—nature being conceived negatively as a nonpurposeful, nonaxiological order. They experienced themselves as utterly grounded, and without any ability to emerge from that ground. At the same time—and this was simply the obverse side of the same perception—people began to see themselves as free, but in a new and terrifying way: free not in the sense of being in control of their destinies, where freedom is construed as a freedom from external constraint, but rather free in the sense of "for nothing," "for free," where freedom is the vast, compelling ground in which we are caught, where life is simply given, for no transcending reason or end.

In chapter 3, I discuss a response to this cultural collapse, a carefully constructed if somewhat manic reaction to the prior depression. Here again I use standard assessments of the antimodern and imperialistic urges that surfaced in America at the turn of the century, what has been called in another context America's complex of "terminal wistfulness."[7] I attempt to evaluate, however, the genuineness of this cultural renovation, the extent to which it offered an honest way out of the earlier dilemma. Did the cultural reconstruction constitute a recovery from or only a continuing cover for the problems that had been exposed in the years following the Civil War?

My conclusion is that the cultural revival was at heart a decadent redescription which denied, and hence deepened, the problem of a self without foundations. What was developed toward the end of the nineteenth century was a historical romance of the self, a narrative built on a call to frenzied action and on rhetoric about living the heroic life. That romance amounted to little more than a means of forgetfulness and escape. It took the recognition of the loss of foundations as a justification for the assertion of the old cultural norms by force; more subtly, and more dangerously, it manipulated the perception of freedom as a determining ground— the perception that we simply do what we will—into the illusory assertion that we can do whatever we want. Here again James enters into the discussion, for he saw through this illusion both in the culture and in his own early work. In turn, he took the major step in his thought away from notions of a strong, assertive, and romanticized self toward an essentially converted self who lived religiously—that is, with a sense of responsibility to rather than control over the free play of forces by which it was bound.

All of this cultural analysis may seem at times to be moving far afield from the specifics of James's writings, and even farther from the task of intellectual history that is primary to my work on James. This, however, is not the case; indeed, I believe it brings us more fully back to both. Very simply, it brings us back to James's writings because it never really leaves them. Internally, it gives us a broad view of all that informed his work; externally, it gives us a sense of his conversation partners and their problems, their resolutions, and their needs. And it brings us back to the story of James's thought in that it makes sensible what some have described as his illogic, "sheer carelessness," and confusion.[8] Seen in the light of his culture, the odd moves that James made in his thought begin to come clear. Viewed from the perspective of the shifting cultural scene, the shifts in James's writings from one subject to another and from one mode of thought to the next cease to seem so arbitrary and abrupt.

To begin with, James's early writings find both their location and their pattern in the cultural collapse of the post–Civil War era. As I discuss in chapter 2, these early writings, particularly *Principles of Psychology*, were an attempt to make sense of the perceived loss of secure groundings for the self. In the *Principles* James quite literally reinvented the self, or rather redrew the self's dimensions, on the cultural assumption that the self was merely a contingent and immanent phenomenon, just a part of a purposeless natural world. Beginning with a blind, almost mechanistic flow, a series of reflex arcs, James constructed first a baby, then a mature person, and finally a self filled with power, a measure of transcendence and determining sway. Stated in the specific terms of my argument, James attempted to respond to the recognition of the loss of foundations. But he did so in the illusory way that became typical by the end of the century, by emphasizing self-assertion and self-recreation as the means to regaining autonomy and a sense of authenticity.[9]

Again, in James's later writings the cultural revival of the turn of the century provides both the grounding and now the dialogic opponent in his work. As I try to show in chapters 4 and 5, the Gifford lectures (*The Varieties of Religious Experience*), the essays on radical empiricism, *Pragmatism*, and *A Pluralistic Universe* all were attempts to counter the model of aggressive self-assertion of his age. Here I return to my point that toward the end of the nineteenth century, James forged a turn in his work away from the self-descriptions, including his own, put forth in the cultural revival. Having seen the socially ruinous consequences of self-assertions, the false divinizations that lurked at their core, and finally the manner in which they were usually left leveled in the dust, James raised up, in juxtaposition to the predominating self-description, a life of conversion and giving up, of plunging back into experience, of trying to make do with whatever immanent relations obtained. Simply put, James's option was fully to give in to contingency. Rather than try to reestablish the self, he went with its dissolution.[10]

By the end of his career, James had developed a clear alternative to the dominant cultural definitions of the self, an understanding of the self as, again, religious, which is to say bound to forces and powers beyond its control, capable of acting, but acting relationally and responsibly rather than independently. All of these forces and powers lacked ultimacy: they were immanent, within the world; none of them could be said to transcend the contingency of things, the fact that everything was given for free. But forces and powers they were. Indeed, they were as compelling as any absolute God. James depicted a self involved in a world of divinities, albeit divinities of our daily lives. He did not reduce powers to human ideals, as did his culture. In turn, he did not see humans as more than co-creative.

In addition to bringing the cultural sources at work in James's thought into play, my contextual analysis does one thing more: it brings us, surprisingly directly, back to ourselves, to our own contemporary cultural dilemmas, problematics, and discussions, and offers a glimpse of the possibilities and limitations of our current cultural constructions. For when one studies American culture in the late nineteenth century it becomes clear that, despite the significant differences between then and now, we continue to be caught by the same fundamental problems and issues, the same failures of cultural definitions, and the same inability to let go of them and genuinely begin again. The cultural collapse that began at the close of the Civil War remains definitive of our current situation: our present is only an extended and exacerbated past, now at its end stage but qualitatively the same. Centuries have a way of setting up boundaries between one era and the next. In this case the boundary between us and the nineteenth century should not be respected overmuch.

In the first five chapters of this book, mirrorings of the present in the past remain, for the most part, implicit. Only in the concluding chapter, where I examine the ways in which, after James's death, his work was taken up, altered, accepted, and rejected, is there an explicit discussion of the continuance of James's age into our own. Throughout, however, what I argue either implicitly or explicitly about our age is that middle class American culture continues to be caught in the problems that result from recognizing the lack of foundations. We have seen through our old cultural definitions: that knowledge can be well founded and that reason can transcend; that our sciences can be neutral and our evaluations value-free; that our experience can be original and autonomous, not reducible to something else. Indeed, we have sharpened the recognition of those old definitions' failures. But we have continued, for the most part, only to be debilitated by that recognition. We have not arrived at responses that are adequate either to the terms of the problem or to the possibilities that may lie within it.

To be sure, as I explain in detail in the final chapter, a range of responses has been made and alternatives proposed. Two types of responses, however, have tended to predominate in American culture since the time of James's death. In the first there is a move to deny the nonfoundational point altogether and to reassert by various means (idealistic, scientistic, even spiritualistic) what amounts to a realist perspective and position. Here the attempt is made to resurrect the Platonic dream of a real world waiting to be found: there is a concern to continue the project of establishing objective groundings for our holdings and our claims; there is an emphasis on constructing correspondences between what we know and the "facts." In the second response, by contrast, there is acceptance of the need to take a nonfoundationalist stance, but denial that the adoption of such a stance poses any particular problems. Here the realist project of world finding is replaced by a liberal, poetic project of creative, human world making. Contingency is interpreted to mean that "there is nothing deep down inside us except what we have put there outselves." The recognition of contingency, in turn, is made the basis for completion of the Enlightenment project of freeing the human person from artificial dependence and constraint.[11]

Both of these responses have points that need to be understood and affirmed. For their part the realists, or world finders, see clearly the threats of nihilism, moral aphasia, and bad relativism that lurk at the door when foundations are let go. They know the tragedy that is often the underside of an unfettered life, the pain that can result from living without any bindings other than to oneself. They perceive the need for some sense of cultural authority, without which, they argue, there is only "the assertion of arbitrary wills, masked by moral fictions, managed by bureaucrats."[12] Liberal and poetic world makers, in turn, have the wisdom to recognize that ultimacy and final authority may be epistemological, if not also ontological, impossibilities. They argue, quite rightly, that despite other needs we may have, we also need to learn how to get along without worship of absolutes. They see the fanaticism that can come with claims to final authority and with positions based on a sure and certain knowledge of the "truth."

Despite the merits of these two responses, however, both continue to reproduce the kind of illusory self-understandings that were characteristic of the late nineteenth century. They both try to salvage from contingency the self of autonomy, independence, and control, the separative, finally superior self whose goal is to be free from "the brutish life of subjection to given conditions."[13] The realist's effort to secure a certain ground of correspondence, the liberal's independently creative stance: both of these constitute attempts to go beyond contingency, to overcome the lack of foundations for the life of the self. In turn, neither sees fit to go along with what, finally, an honest understanding of contingency may entail, namely, that the self in charge of its destiny must relinquish its privileged place apart from the rest of the world.

My criticism here, it should be added, is not just mine alone. In the final chapter, as I detail the analysis I have just outlined, I do so with the help of others, some working from within the pragmatist tradition, others working from a feminist perspective. This is to say that I take as at least potential allies those people who see the dominant cultural constructions as but one more attempt to hang on to notions of intentional subjectivity, where the goal of life is "to be outstanding," that is, to stand over against the web of our environing field. In turn, it is to say that I am attempting to contribute to their reconstructions and revisionings of the self, in which the self is construed not separatively but along with everything else, where "the essential religious insight . . . is to know that we are no more valuable to the life of the universe than a field flowering in the color purple, than rivers flowing, than a crab picking its way across the sand—and no less."[14]

Again it might seem that I have moved far afield from James, but that is not the case. Rather I have come in a roundabout way to the third and last thing that this book on James is about, the prospective purpose of my retrospective glance. I also have arrived at the argument that underlies the whole of the book, namely, that James's understanding of the cultural problems of his age, his criticism of available cultural strategies, and his own alternative proposals have more than historical significance; indeed, they may be of direct help to us. Intellectual history and historical-cultural analysis both give way here to a comment on contemporary bourgeois American life. The central point is that James's understanding and avowal of a religious way of being, a way based on that peculiar kind of freedom that is born of submission to and respect for ties that are binding, is an understanding that we need to achieve and an avowal that we need to make if we are genuinely and constructively to learn to get along in a world without foundations.

The source of James's present relevance lies in the thoroughness of and integrity with which he held on to his understanding that we live in a nonfoundational world. If, by the end of his career, James gave us a way to talk about and live in that world religiously, it was done with honesty, flush against the fact that all we do lacks final grounding. James knew the falsity of the reality-appearance distinction, and the falsity of attempts to rebuild the modern world on that Old World base. As I have said, his first and probably his central work, *The Principles of Psychology*, takes as its starting point and thesis the unqualified contingency of things. All of his subsequent work holds to and enlarges upon that nonfoundational point.

James also understood the need to root out all false worship and pretense. He knew, as the liberal world maker reiterates today, that to posit a realm of absolutes even at the level of practical postulates was just an uncritical evasion of the facts. However much we might need them, James recognized, pragmatically considered there were no ultimate authorities available to hold us in line. Even in his most traditionally theistic moments, when he spoke about his theory of a "piecemeal supernaturalism," James upheld the antiabsolutist, antifoundationalist view. His work was at one with the option of trying to get along without treating anything as other than a product of contingency and time.

But James also knew that self-assertion was not the way to get along. Here his understanding is of value in helping us out of the major pitfall of the liberal position, for he saw through what is today the liberal's hidden agenda in calling for an assertive self-redescription, understood that this simply brought in by the back door what had been barred at the gate. Respect for the contingency of things did not mean that there was nothing at work in the world except what we posited and made. To understand contingency in that sense was to continue to hold ourselves out as the sole creators of our worlds. In turn, it was to continue to see the human person as transcending and supreme.

Here James began to appreciate the position of today's realists. He raised a call for receptivity and openness, for a counter to the complacency and susceptibility to decadent irresponsibility in the liberal's heroic strong self. In turn, he raised a call for a kind of humility, a due appreciation of the integrity of the world, and a recognition of the fact that we not only make up worlds but also, and always, find ourselves in worlds that are not just of our making. James fully let go of the controlling underside of the self, dissolved the ego fantasy of being able to gain a standing point beyond the compulsiveness of the fray. He talked of the self as always and incurably involved in a web of relations within which it could, at most, play its part badly or well. He saw the self not as an independent storyteller, nor as a reweaver of tales, but as a being whose mission in life was always a submission, a being in, through, and out of whom stories were told.

This recognition of how thoroughly the self was embedded in a relational world brought James to an appreciation of the realist's religious insight that human life has integrity only when it is lived responsively and responsibly, that is, with an awareness of and respect for the ties that at any given point are binding. He understood the logic behind the realist desire to discern the correlations and correspondences between the self and all that was at work "out there." More to the point, he recognized the importance of the realist's stress on the fact that "we are finite, limited, and conditioned beings who owe our existence to forces beyond our control and who exercise whatever freedom we have only under circumstances we have not authored."[15] But again, James did not let that recognition slip over into a reassertion of absolutes or of a transcendent controlling realm. With the realist, James understood that some of who we are, and indeed sometimes who we are, are more compelling powers which may have the right to be called gods. But unlike the realist, James held that even the seemingly ultimate powers in life are grounded, as we are, in contingency. Thus they are worthy of respect and recognition but not of worship or blind obedience. They too take their part in submission to the free relational play.

The upshot of James's understandings, and in turn their full relevance for us, is that they cut through some of the usual boundaries of our perspectives. James's thought provides a way to hold on to the nonfoundational wisdom of the liberal and at the same time the relational insight and, at its heart, the religious concern of the realist. It does so, moreover, in a way that lets go of the limitations inherent in their respective positions, the privileges and transcendences that lurk at their core. As a result, James's thought gives what both of those options aim for, but neither of them alone is quite able to achieve: namely, a respect for and understanding of life as rooted in and sustained by responsibility and interrelations, or, more simply put, a way to live freely without any illusion that freedom is something we possess or can control. All of that, I believe, warrants our attention, and perhaps our avowal. It will repay us to investigate and hear again what James had, and has, to say.

I

THE EARLY YEARS:
1865–1890

1

A Presence of Absence

Here is the first thing of which I retain a clear remembrance. I was alone, and already a prey to permanent visual trouble, when I was suddenly seized with a visual trouble infinitely more prounounced. Objects grew small and receded to infinite distances—men and things together. I was myself immeasurably far away. I looked about me with terror and astonishment; the world was escaping from me . . . I remarked at the same time that my voice was extremely far away from me, that it sounded no longer as if mine. I struck the ground with my foot, and perceived its resistance; but this resistance seemed illusory—not that the soil was soft, but that the weight of my body was reduced to almost nothing. I had the feeling of being without weight. In addition to being so distant, objects appeared to me flat. When I spoke with anyone, I saw him like an image cut out of paper with no relief. . . . This sensation lasted intermittently for two years. . . . Constantly it seemed as if my legs did not belong to me. It was almost as bad with my arms. As for my head, it seemed no longer to exist. . . . I appeared to myself to act automatically, by an impulsion foreign to myself. . . . I had an ardent desire to see my old world again, to get back to my old self.

William James, *The Principles of Psychology*

And will he not come again?
And will he not come again?
No, no, he is dead,
Go to thy death-bed,
He will never come again.
His beard as white as snow.

17

All flaxen, was his poll:
He is gone, he is gone,
And we cast away moan,
God ha' mercy on his soul!
William Shakespeare, *Hamlet*

By the late 1860s, the cultural construction supporting America's middle class was on the verge of giving out. "Neurasthenia,"[1] what in popular terms was called a failure of nerve, had become the cultural mode, so much so that Congress convened a committee to investigate its causes and ramifications. It was held as the distinguishing mark of a distinctively American way of living. Those who could afford the luxury sought refuge in remedies of rest and recline; the gospel of relaxation was called in to take over for the now outmoded gospel of strenuous effort. Even the landscape seemed to have altered, as if to accommodate the needs of the weary. Sprinkled across the burned-over districts of revivalistic conflagration there suddenly appeared hot springs, health spas, and water cure resorts.

In the decades leading up to the 1860s, the seat of American culture had been the anxious bench, that symbolic locus not only of a commerce with God but of a whole system of productive enterprise. Now it was the S-shaped couch by the parlor window that was the central prop: its curvilinear sweep, mirroring the invalid body, was expressive of a culture in which gentle nurture had overcome the harshness of a sudden conversion, in which a feeling of well-being rather than the violence of one's convulsions was the measure of the good. From the anxious bench to taking to bed. As William James wrote in a letter to his brother Henry on February 1, 1870: "[I]t seems to me that all a man has to depend on in this world is, in the last resort, mere brute power of resistance."[2]

There was, of course, more to be noted than the culture's collapse. Whatever "blood-dimmed tides" had risen, there had been, after all, a Union victory in the Civil War. The Union's interests had been preserved, and opportunities abounded for their furtherance. Abundance, the promised reward for those who had redeemed the founders' vision of the nation, seemed imminent if not aleady arrived. "We not only wear better heads," said Henry Ward Beecher, "but we have better bellies, with better food in them. We also have better clothes now. In other words, the art of living healthily has advanced immensely."[3]

But even Beecher had to admit that there were those who "are born to see the devil of melancholy, they would see him sitting in the very door of heaven, methinks."[4] Along with the images of national expansion, technological outbuilding, and corporational upbuilding (such as the Corliss engine and the office building) there were always, it seemed, competing and more compelling images of a world out of control: a socially slipping educated elite; a growing and restive class of urban poor; a recurring failure of business to capitalize on its opportunities. And there were also the casualties of the war: soldiers who, whether victorious or not, returned strangely defeated; the remnants of families; those who had not fought and lived with the reproof, as James put it: "Hang yourself, brave Crillon. We fought at Arques, and you were not there."[5] In the years following the Civil War, three American translations of the *Divine Comedy* appeared. In Lewis Mumford's words, "That terrible, rapturous celebration of the dead was keyed to the best temper of the brown decades."[6]

The nation seemed to many to be caught in a cul-de-sac, one of those blind alleys of history into which wars so often seem to lead. More to the point, it had lost its sense of ultimate grounding, its understanding that American life was well founded. Before the Civil War the rhetoric of the nation had been formed around phrases about the founding fathers, the founders' vision, and so forth. By the end of the war these phrases had been dropped: the founding fathers had become merely the forefathers; no one really believed that the war had preserved their vision, or if they did, they knew that vision was far from ideal. Simply put, the country was becoming aware just how fully contingent the project of independence was and how terrifying freedom could be. Hard lessons were being learned about what it meant to live of, by, and for the people.

It would have been better if the culture could simply have been written off as dead, if the consensus had been that something of value had been permanently lost rather than that something deeply flawed persisted. But in this case the old avenues of aspiration remained in place, even though they had been seen through and had lost their force. And dreams with solid images still were recorded, even though they were written, "as it were, on things that exist not."[7] To understand the cultural crisis of the postwar years is to grasp the fact of the culture's deep ambivalence. As Abraham Lincoln said five days before his death, quoting from *Macbeth* for a group of friends: "Better be with the dead, / Whom we, to gain our peace, have sent to peace, / Than on the torture of the mind to lie / In restless ecstasy."[8]

What, at the heart of things, occurred in the 1860s was that the complex of cultural definitions supporting self-identity lost their moorings and their ground of meanings. They remained in use, but increasingly were seen as little more than platitudes. The lingering pall of the war, urbanization, and industrialization; a scientific and technological revolution; an increasingly impersonal and bureau-cratized social order: all of these placed strains on the cultural pictures of the self. They gave the lie to these images' certainty and depth. America's absolutism of the individual, with the self set squarely and independently at life's center stage, suddenly lost its meaning. New, decadent images of the human person began to compete with the old definitions, spanning the spectrum from a dead and purposelessly determined self to a self disordered and in disarray.

Symptomatic of the breakdown was the philosophical agenda of Boston's Metaphysical Club of the 1870s (the core of which con-sisted of Oliver Wendell Holmes the younger, Chauncey Wright, Charles Peirce, and William James): tychism, naturalism, varieties of fatalism, and the realism of chance. On a more popular level, essayists and novelists lamented the fact of the excluded middle ground, the sudden impotence of formerly reliable models and images. "Going hungry, hopeless, blinded, I came away empty, uncomforted, groping," says the heroine of Elizabeth Stuart Phelps's novel *The Gates Ajar*, as she reflects on a meeting with her minister. "He gave me glittering generalities, cold commonplace, vagueness, unreality, a God and a future at which I sat and shiv-ered."[9]

One of the first definitions to lose its meaning was that of social stability, the notion that the country had a standing and permanent order and, more to the point, that the self belonged in a place. The erosion of this societal definition had begun as early as the 1840s, when, under the enticements of a nationally spreading marketplace, households that had previously remained settled and unitary started breaking up and moving away. Suddenly there was a spate of essays and treatises on the domestic life, headed by Horace Bushnell's 1847 publication of *Discourses on Christian Nurture*.[10] The Civil War only exacerbated the problems of the shifting social scene: it reshuffled society; it opened access to new areas of the country and distributed family members to new places; it preserved the Union but at the expense of regional unity. Above all there was the threat to stability posed by the steady influx of immigrants, who not only added a variety of cultural alternatives and competing institutions but also, because of the vagaries of economics and industrial development, created an image of a society in constant transition.[11]

To some with an investment in the official images of social solidity, the postwar society seemed just about spent, on the verge of a "kind of mental and moral chaos, in which many of the fundamental rules of living . . . seem in imminent risk of disappearing totally."[12] To others the threat was exactly the opposite, that social definition was giving way to the leveling laws of statistics, to the determinism of numbers and quantity. "Murmurs of many voices in the air / Denounce us as degenerate," wrote James Russell Lowell in his "Ode for the Fourth of July, 1876." "Is this the country that we dreamed in youth, / Where wisdom and not numbers should have weight?"[13]

Whichever way opinion ran, there was agreement that ideas of societal order had become all too indefinite. Even the most uncompromising institutional pronouncements conceded the fact of change in their denials and reaffirmations. "This is a Christian republic," declared a writer in a Presbyterian journal. "If anyone coming among us, finds that this arrangement is uncomfortable, perhaps he will do well to try some other country."[14] Statements such as this contained more bravado than substance; everyone knew that the only backing they had was force. And these were assertions based not on the assumption of a stable definition, but on the hope that the breakdown of definitions might be held to a minimum. The damage had already been done.

The disintegration of definitions of social stability might not have caused such perturbation had it not been linked to other declines and failures. Movement, after all, does not need to be vexing, provided it offers some sense of direction and adventure. But along with the breakdown of the social definitions came a decline in clarity of the point and direction of individual life. Fewer people could profess the creed "All bound as is befitting each—all surely going somewhere."[15] America's errand suddenly seemed to have come to an end; it became increasingly difficult to conceive of life in the optative mood. Even Walt Whitman finally had to admit that the times had changed, that the days of voyaging might be over.

> In some unused lagoon, some nameless bay,
> On sluggish, lonesome waters, anchor'd near the shore,
> An old dismasted, gray and batter'd ship, disabled, done,
> After free voyages to all the seas of earth,
> haul'd up at last and hawser'd tight,
> Lies rusting, mouldering.[16]

Hand in hand with this loss of the optative sense was a hardening of cultural images of plasticity, of the depiction of the self as open and responsive to the new. As the deterministic logic of the industrial and natural sciences came to dominate America's pictures of reality, space, time, and power lost their sovereign sway. Where formerly these had served as sacred, founding conditions of the self's life, now they appeared arbitrary and conditioned. "God's time" and "local time" became the standard zones of a mechanical timekeeper. The expansiveness of space was reduced to scheduled points of arrival and departure. And human work ceased to be defined in terms of spontaneous action: labor was depicted according to units of measurement; human effort was conceived as mechanical, as automatic rather than creative.[17]

"Hitch your wagon to a star," Emerson had written in "Society and Solitude," but increasingly after the war Americans reversed the images and, as in the confatal argument, stars were hitched to wagons. Aspirations and flights of imagination were repeatedly reduced to a biological, dead beating flow. Memories, dreams, and the imaginings of the soul were, as Oliver Wendell Holmes stated in 1870, "essentially mechanical and necessary." It was no wonder that movement had lost its sense of exhilaration: not only had the ship of flight been dismasted, but the captain had lost control.[18]

This loss of a sense of plasticity meant that the vital character of life appeared to be in jeopardy, and even more so the ability to experience life directly, to live, as Emerson put it, at firsthand. Over and again the complaint was raised that Americans were quite literally out of touch with life, that human activity had become detached both from formal productive purposes and from the final ends of products. Cultural critics decried what they saw as a change from a society of enterprise, of full engagement in life's tasks, to a society of maintenance in which action was artificial, simply a matter of going through the motions. "Our land is now full of motorpathic institutions to which women are sent at great expense to have hired operators stretch and exercise their inactive muscles," wrote Harriet Beecher Stowe in "The Lady Who Does Her Own Work." And then she compared the present "torpid" age to an earlier age of enterprise: "I will venture to say that our grandmothers in a week went over every movement that any gymnast had invented, and went over them to some productive purpose too."[19]

There was much more, of course, to the loss of firsthand life than ennui and enervation, and the sources of the problem ran far deeper than the inactivity of the privileged. As society shifted from an entrepreneurial to an organizational and corporational structure, images of life as alienated began to replace those depicting life as integral and of a piece. The development and application of management techniques divorced decision making from labor: workers had their decisions made from afar, while managers had their physical work reduced to recreation. And the acceptance of specialization and departmentalization as necessary ways of life created a disjunction between parts and the whole; activity was depicted as piecemeal, without a sense of overarching unity. Nowhere, or so it seemed, could a person be wholly involved in the entirety of a process. The integrity of the self seemed, very literally, to have split apart.

With technical rationality gaining ascendancy in the culture, the consent of the human, the will to do or not, seemed beside the point. To be sure the culture continued to hold out images of self-determination—as in the almost medieval depictions of the autonomous inventor—but there was usually a catch. That is, the more one lived a life of self-determination, the more one locked oneself into a system designed to deprive the will of its determining power. Thomas Edison, who, as the "Wizard of Menlo Park," seemed the very embodiment of an entrepreneurial past, put forth products from his "research laboratory" that furthered the distance between the self and life, made the will to act a moot point. Discussing the development of the phonograph, Edison listed as *fait accomplis*:

> The captivity of all manner of sound-waves heretofore designated as fugitive, and their permanent retention. . . . Their reproduction with all their original characteristics at will, without the presence or consent of the original source. . . . Indefinite multiplication and preservation of such sounds, without regard to the existence or non-existence of the original source.[20]

Edison, of course, intended nothing bad by his statements; his optimism blinded him to the ominous side of his own insight. He viewed his work as a means of revitalizing his age, and his inventions as harbingers of a cultural system in which control could be defined by the capacity to have goods rather than to produce them. He did not seem to notice that the possession of a reproduction might appear to some a poor substitute for the power of origination. It escaped him that his language of technocracy, with its emphasis on captivity and retention and its disregard for human productive sources, sounded like the language of a slave society.

Other more wary observers saw in such statements what Edison refused to see; they stood before the inventions of the age like Amish before a camera. What they feared was that the ordinary facts of existence could express no longer the fundamental truths of the striving human spirit but only the machinations of a technological system. As they saw it, mechanization was taking command of the culture's mythology: stories centering on the autonomous self were being replaced by tales about the omnipotence of the machine.

Frequently this fear was expressed in the complaint that life had been drained of its heroic aspects. Where formerly stories had depicted humanity prevailing over the necessities of living, now, with the advance of civilization, the best that could be said was that the human might endure. "I am quite aware," Elizabeth Stuart Phelps interjected in "The Tenth of January," "that according to all romantic precedents, this conduct was quite preposterous." But,

Phelps went on, her main character could not be a heroine in the expected sense of the word; in turn, her story could not be written in the usual pattern of struggle and release, suffering and overcoming. The protagonist provided scant material by which the reader could be overcome with a "sense of poetic justice and the eternal fitness of things." "[A]s the biographer of this simple factory girl," Phelps concluded, "[I] am offered few advantages."[21]

Concomitant with the felt decline in heroic material was the sense that nature had lost its role as the ground and inspirational center for the heroic self's life. Simply put, nature was increasingly seen not as alive but as dead, as only a resource or as property to be owned. "What a glorious place this must have been for lovers' strolls," remarks James Richardson in "Travelling by Telegraph," as if remembering a natural world he no longer either knew or believed in. "That shows how your mind runs," comes a rebuke; "I was thinking what splendid timber ties these oaks would make." And then the scene shifts abruptly; the disputants board a train to investigate factories and mill towns in the hope, which is never realized, that they might offer a new stage for heroic activity.[22]

Some of this may seem trivial, the carping criticism of those who are forced to take their sentimentality with a touch of realism. And there is something to this view, because part of the initial American reaction to the loss of self-definitions was to be sentimental. But sentimentality is a symptom of a deeper disease: if one can stand it long enough to understand it, it shows itself to be not just feigned emotion but the end stage of vitality. There is no depth to sentimentality because nothing inspires more deeply. The sentimentality of the post–Civil War era should be understood as a mark of the decay in the foundations of America's images of the self.

The loss of stability and plasticity, of purpose, immediacy, and self-determination—all of this struck bottom against a disintegrating framework of religious meaning, a crumbling definition of the ultimate dimension of the self. The Protestant religious structure, which had given self-definitions their correspondences to an absolute ground, was failing to respond convincingly to the questions posed by the cultural crisis. Where it might have given solidity to the thinning cultural images, it heightened the feeling of contingency. When it was supposed to provide alternatives to the eroding pictures of the self, it offered only one more instance of cultural foundations being uprooted. Above all, when it should have been preparing a way to salvation, it simply held out obscure images of uncertain paths, further examples of blocked avenues of aspiration. Phillips Brooks put the point well in a sermon titled "The Light of the World": "A sense of foreignness and unnaturalness and strangeness lies like a fog across the entrance of the divine country; a certain wonder whether I, a man, have any business there, an unreality about it all; a break and a gulf between what the world is and what we know it ought to be."[23]

The most outward members of the religious framework to have faltered were the institutional structures. In the eyes of many the churches no longer were spiritual havens, bulwarks for the self against the rising tide of social instability, but rather another site of spiritual homelessness. Some complained that the ways and means of the religious institutions were insufficient to meet the needs of a complex, urbanizing society. They agreed with the urban revivalist Dwight Moody, who concluded after a decade of evangelization in the cities that the "simple message" of the churches no longer could resolve "the problems connected with industrialization."[24]

According to many observers, however, the problem was not that the Protestant institutional order had collapsed, nor that it had lost its hegemony in the culture; the lively experiment, while embattled and shaken here and there, nevertheless was still the story of a continuing success. Indeed, many saw that Protestantism had extended its control, setting the pattern not only for its own organization but for the corporate organization of society. The difficulty had less to do with a lack of growth on the part of religious institutions than with the fact of their growth, and with the way they seemed to go on growing regardless of, and many times at the expense of, the needs and wants of believers and society.

Thus, while historical hindsight may afford a view of religion as incorporated into a secularizing national order, to many at the time the situation seemed much more fluid, with religious institutions sometimes playing the part of unwitting victims but also, and perhaps more often, consciously contributing to a depersonalizing social system.[25] In "The City Without a Church," Henry Drummond flatly declared "Church type" religion to be "an elaborate evasion" unrelated to the lives of most people.[26] Others made sim-

ilar charges, attributing the religious institutions' lack of respon-
siveness to cultural questions to an increasing adherence to a bureaucratic mentality. "Some of our congregations compete like
rival tradesmen," said Rabbi Isaac Wise. "Synagogues have grown
to be business corporations." And when Swami Vivekananda, having told a group of listeners that he had faced his greatest temptation in America, was asked, "Who is she?" he replied: "Oh, it is not
a lady, it is organization."[27]

There was criticism from the other side as well that religious
institutions were exacerbating the problem of social instability by
insisting on specialization and the separation of denominations. "Is
the great family of man divided?" asked the Anglo-Catholic James
DeKoven. "The Christianity which is to remedy this is still more
divided than the human race itself."[28] Charles Briggs of Union
Theological Seminary in New York stated the point even more
bluntly, claiming that the churches had forfeited their "authority
as a divine institution" in large measure because of their insistence
on denominationalism, "the great sin and curse of the modern
Church."[29] And various members of the scientific community
voiced their concern that Protestant patterns of religious formation, "with the subdivision into sects which has sprung from it, is
an element in the causation of the nervous diseases of our time."[30]

Whichever way the criticism ran, the common accusation was
that the churches were giving far less than they were taking. Neither
union nor denominationalism seemed capable of offering a religious definition of stability, a point of certainty amid the social
flux. Or rather, the price to be paid for either alternative was too
steep. Church union offered stability, but at the cost of leveling
differences; it fostered an institutional structure in which the church
became simply one more of the "vast, unmeasured forces [that]
hold us in their hands."[31] Denominationalism, while preserving the
sense of difference and control, contributed to a grinding competition and consigned religious institutions to an increasingly special-
ized and circumscribed sphere of influence. Neither offered a secure
framework for understanding the self; together they seemed only to
be repeating the pattern by which the self was being split up and
leveled down.

Feelings of vagueness were not wholly attributable to the problems and changes in the institutional life of the churches; institu-

tional structures provided only a portion of the framework for the Protestant pattern of religious life that dominated American culture. Of equal importance were the theological and ethical structures of what was loosely labeled Calvinist theology, which meant, above all else, depictions of the relationship between human and divine activity. In the decades that embraced the Civil War, central tenets about the self and God came under close scrutiny and were found wanting. Where formerly they had been seen as sure guides, now they were regarded as inadequate and inauthentic, as fostering the very problems of self-definition they were supposed to be answering.

For some the Calvinist conceptions of God and self were concepts whose time had passed, dead symbols that neither represented the eternal truths nor made sense in terms of contemporary issues and dilemmas. Oliver Wendell Holmes, one of the more conservative critics of Calvinism, saw the aging Edwardsean definitions as unnecessary burdens on the culture: the language of sin and guilt, of regeneration and saintliness, was inefficient and unproductive; the terms of science, with definitions based on conceptions of behavior, were more specific and much better suited to the needs of the age. The point for Holmes was not that Calvinism was wrong so much as that it was outworn, a dessicated shell that needed to be sloughed off. To continue under the Calvinist system was like living under the tutelage of one's ancestors; it created a society in which "live folks are just dead folks warmed over."[32]

To others, however, it was not the outdatedness of Calvinism that was problematic but its accommodation to modern thinking.[33] These observers viewed even the conservative progressivism of a Holmes as illustrative of a dangerous tendency in religious thought in which the ethical tenets of Calvinism were being softened into a liberal creed that had no force or conviction. It was no wonder that Calvinism was failing to offer alternatives to the improverished images of the individual and the societal self: its sense of the meaning and rigorousness of life had been watered down to the point where any action seemed viable but no action seemed vital. "The force by which the world has chiefly grown hitherto is the love of excellence for its own sake, the feeling of obligation to try to make things better," wrote Jonathan Baxter Harrison. He went on to warn that the reassertion of an ethical definition of the self based on disinterested benevolence was the only way to recover the authentic foundations of human life and action. "But," he concluded, "it is to be confessed that these are considerations of little weight with the optimism of our time."[34]

Still others scoffed at the notion that the Calvinist conceptions had suffered a decline at all. They were as strong as they had ever been, and as dehumanizing as ever. "History shows," wrote Elizabeth Cady Stanton in *North American Review*, "that the moral degradation of woman is due more to theological superstitions than to all other influences together,"[35] echoing a complaint raised by many groups for whom the Calvinist definition of human life meant a loss of autonomy, exclusion, and marginalization. Theological definitions of the self were even blamed for the general melancholia of the era. As John Girdner wrote in an article titled "Theology and Insanity": "[A] careful study of the history of mental diseases amply proves that . . . the theologies of man have caused so many minds to give way and settled delusions and hallucinations of a so-called religious type."[36]

Whatever the specific complaint may have been, there was a common recognition that theological structures of belief were completely unable to shore up the self. Liberalism and the various progressive orthodoxies provided a measure of self-definition with their notions of responsible social action; they had taken the first steps toward a new cultural definition in which authenticity would be redefined in terms of a social self, and by which solidity could be gained through images of what was usually called the "brotherhood of man."[37] Their redefinitions, however, seemed awfully shallow: it was never quite clear just who was meant by the brotherhood (although it was fairly clear who was not); these images were easily manipulated. And because their definitions squared neither with the old light verities nor with the new light truths of modern science but tried to straddle both, they appeared to many to be without depth, to lack clear, objective foundation.

Although the institutional and theological structures of belief were failing, the possibility remained that integrity could be found in private structures of religious practice. America's religious culture, after all, had always put as much stock in patterns of privatization as in patterns of institutionalization, had tried to maintain a balance between frameworks of religious meaning based on political structures and sources of religious meaning derived from personal and communal experience. Private avenues of religiosity had long been the wellspring of an open and intimate universe, the locus of the security of the truth. As long as these remained open, there was at least a potential response to the overdetermined images of the self offered by the rest of the culture.

Personal and communal religiosity, however, also disintegrated, or rather lost its foundations and supports and was cut loose to fend for itself. Mainstream religious institutions continued to show concern for the private patterns of devotion, but much of the time their efforts were aimed at restructuring the personal and communal arenas into impersonal links in an organizational chain.[38] More important, perhaps, than the loss of the church's support was the loss of support by the scientific community, whose revolution had been a piece with the revolution of the saints, and whose assumptions about the power and prerogatives of direct observation, investigation, and experience had supported personal patterns of piety.[39] When the scientists shifted their allegiance to the corporate and industrial orders, turned coats, and became priests of the secular cloth, they took with them the logic and language that had given warrant and expression to the private structures of belief.

What appeared to be left was a religious heart without imagination, patterns of piety without convincing expression or authority. Personal and communal religious credentials suddenly seemed shaky, without sufficient backing. Where formerly personal religious claims had been seen as prophetic, as harbingers of a new age, now they were accused of being anachronistic remnants of a premodern past. Promoters of the private realm were capable only of defensive responses; they appeared unable to get beyond an almost conspiratorial feeling that "the attempt is being made, with singular vigor and persistence, to reduce the life of Christian people to those beggarly limits of experience and aspiration."[40]

Symptomatic of the breakdown in the private structures of belief was the anxiety expressed about private patterns of meditation, for example, about the fruitfulness of individual and communal Bible reading given the higher biblical criticism that had been imported from Europe.[41] Elizabeth Stuart Phelps, who, as the granddaughter of the biblical scholar Moses Stuart, knew as well as most popular writers the intricacies of the new science of criticism and of "that frowning original Greek," nevertheless lamented the sense of futility about private inspirational reading of the Bible. "No sooner do I find a pretty verse that is exactly what I want, then up hops a commentator, and says, this isn't according to text, and means something entirely different; and Barnes says this, and Stuart believes that, and Olshausen has demonstrated the other, and very ignorant it is in you, too, not to know it."[42] Others interested in interpreting the Scriptures for their social paradigms and understandings saw their readings rendered impotent by the keepers of the critical keys, who charged that the models they were raising were highly suspect, and most probably unhistorical.[43]

Anxiety about the reductionism of the biblical sciences was not, of course, the only symptom of the fading private structures; the loudest cries of alarm were raised about the inroads on personal belief being made by the natural sciences. Psychology, biology, the whole of "medical materialism" was challenging not only the right of the untrained to religious claims but the deeper notion that the self was reflective of a higher order. Whereas biblical scholars had found personal experience and inspiration of doubtful value, here they were being called a sham and a fraud. What is important, however, is that once more there were no ready replies to the charge that human personality was simply the sum of its own natural tendencies; the power of definition appeared to belong to those who asserted that

> God's love, we are now taught, is no more than the mere yearning of the sad human heart to find a living expression . . . while the hope of immortality, by the same rule, is the vain effort of that faculty of our nature which looks "before and after" to construct a future which may sooth its imagination, but which is baseless and fruitless as its wildest dream.[44]

"If the universe were only a set of facts," said Boston University's Borden Bowne, "it would have nothing in it to awaken wonder, enthusiasm, and reverence. . . . Such a universe would not be worth knowing."[45] So ran the customary apology for private religiosity; it was as if the best that could be said was that, given the human need for a mysterious and open universe, the authority of the scoffers would one day wane and religion would reassert its primacy. The problem with apologies such as these, and the reason they so often fell on deaf ears, was that they skirted the issues that needed to be resolved. The dilemma posed by the cultural crisis was to find a way to see human life and activity as something well founded, as something more than contingent and matter-of-fact. Wistful statements such as Bowne's simply answered the question asked about life by repeating it in the indicative. Few needed to be told that a world without wonder or purpose would be without meaning.

On a somewhat deeper level, defenders of the religious life failed to address the heart of the problem, which concerned the status of religious claims and the reasons why they should be given credence at all. Reminders about the quality of religious experience, and stern admonitions that scientific facts amounted to a rather paltry sum without the addition of the facts of faith, did, of course, have their point, as well as some effect. But the quality of religious experience was moot unless and until a convincing case could be made for the religious quality of experience.

"Has Deity directly revealed itself to man?" wrote Goldwin Smith in an article titled "The Religious Situation," asking a question that seldom received an answer clearly in the affirmative.[46] The paucity of responses to the question, even from those who held to the vitality of religious life, and the poverty of the responses that were given were indicative of the depth of the cultural crisis in post–Civil War America. Not only had the culture reached an outer, historical limit, hit a point where it could no longer revivify fading definitions of the self or offer plausible alternatives to them. It also had reached a point of inner existential limitation where religious identity dried up, where mechanisms of revival repeatedly failed to revive the spirit, where the self touched bottom not against some indwelling power of ultimacy but against its own inner emptiness. To be sure, stories continued to be told about souls struggling through the labyrinth of religious self-scrutiny, trying to secure their deliverance. The introspective path of pilgrims' progress, which had been prescribed by evangelists from Bunyan to the Awakeners to the Transcendentalists, continued to be followed. The path seemed for the most part, however, only to double back upon itself; self-scrutiny led not to a sense of fulfillment but to lunatic visions and a morbid despair. "By vast pains we mine into the pyramid," wrote Herman Melville. "[B]y horrible gropings we come to the central room; with joy we espy the sarcophagus; but we lift the lid—and no body is there! appallingly vacant as vast is the soul of man."[47]

2

Reweaving the Self

It is written: In the beginning was the Word.
Here I am struck at once. Who will help me on?
I am unable to grant the word such merit,
I must translate it differently
If I am truly illumined by the spirit.
It is written: In the beginning was the Mind.
But why should my pen scour
So quickly ahead? Consider the first line well.
Is it the Mind that effects and creates all things?
It should read: In the beginning was the Power.
Yet, even as I am changing what I have writ,
Something warns me not to abide by it.
The spirit prompts me, I see in a flash what I need,
And write: In the beginning was the Deed!
                    Johann Wolfgang von Goethe, *Faust*

The house of fiction has in short not one window, but a million, a number of possible windows not to be reckoned, rather; every one of which has been pierced, or is still pierceable, in its vast front, by the need of the individual vision and by the pressure of the individual will. These apertures, of dissimilar shape and size, hang so, all together, over the human scene that we might have expected of them a greater sameness of report than we find. They are but windows at the best, mere holes in a dead wall, disconnected, perched aloft; they are not hinged doors opening straight upon life. But they have this mark of their own that at each of them stands a figure with a pair of eyes, or at least with a field glass, which forms, again and again, for observation, a unique instrument, insuring to the person making use of it an impression distinct from every other. He and his neighbors are watching the same show, but one seeing more where the other sees less, one seeing black where the other sees white, one seeing big where the

other sees small, one seeing coarse where the other sees fine.
And so on, and so on; there is fortunately no saying on what,
for the particular pair of eyes, the window may not open;
"fortunately" by reason, precisely, of this incalculability of
range.   Henry James, *Portrait of a Lady*

In 1878 William James contracted with the publisher Henry Holt to
write a textbook on psychology. Although James worked haltingly
at best, and with many a moment wasted (the book took twelve
years to complete), Holt could not have gotten a better author.
James had a knowledge of the then-current psychological methods
and theories which was as broad as any in America. He had studied
under the experimentalists in Germany, and was deeply absorbed in
the Scottish and associationist psychologies. He was in correspondence with the leaders of the French psychiatric school, and a
member of and proselytizer for the Society for Psychical Research.
He was a student of the Darwinists, but one who had learned
his respect for the "facts" from the stuanch anti-Darwinist Louis
Agassiz.[1]

This diversity of knowledge, coupled with the broad outlook it
produced in James, guaranteed the success of *Principles of Psychology*[2] as an academic and scholarly book. What made it a popular
book, however, had less to do with the breadth of James's knowledge than with what reviewers called his peculiarly "human" tone
and approach to his material. To begin with, James made the
psychologists appear all too human. He was constantly reminding
his readers about the "psychologist's fallacy." His text was flagged
with warnings that "at present psychology is in the condition of
physics before Galileo and the laws of motion, of chemistry before
Lavoisier and the notion that mass is preserved in all motion."[3]

This caution about the professional psychologists and the status
of their claims and observations had as its obverse a respect for the
claims of the nonprofessional. James heard evidence customarily
ruled inadmissible. He accepted theoretical considerations from
sources with few if any credentials other than their own experience.
And he valued more highly than the scientist's definitions of prob-

lems those raised by people such as his readers. "The spectator's judgment is sure to miss the root of the matter, and to possess no truth," James stated in a lecture on his psychology. "[W]herever there is conflict of opinion and difference of vision, we are bound to believe that the truer side is the side that feels the more, and not the side that feels the less."[4]

There were some, of course, who condemned James's breach of evidentiary conventions, and who saw his approach in the text as lacking scientific scruples. "The principle of the uncritical acceptance of data," wrote Charles Sanders Peirce in a review of James's text for the *Nation*, "to which Professor James clings, practically amounts to a claim for a new kind of liberty of thought, which would make a complete rupture with accepted methods of psychology and of science in general."[5] And the critics had their point. James not only allowed in the evidence and opinions of the untrained; he went on to hold their facts and stories, raw and unrefined, as ultimate data. "Psychology as So-Called Natural Science" was the disdainful response of Yale's George Trumbull Ladd.[6] It did seem sometimes as if James was only out to prove his contention about belief, namely, that we would believe everything if we could.

Other, less scientifically reverent reviewers, however, saw the point of distinction in James's tactics; they applauded him precisely for his refusal to separate realms. As John Dewey put it, James's decision not to abide by the strict rules of scientific evidence enabled him to investigate "genuine events, events that most persons are too conventional or too literal to note at all."[7] And it was the everyday quality of James's facts—addictions to narcotics, inabilities to get work done, lost limbs (an odd point to dwell on until one recalls the Civil War and the crudity of factory systems and medical practices)—and their commonality with his readers' lives, that elicited the here congratulatory comment from the editor of *Harper's Magazine* that "it must be admitted that he has come dangerously near writing a popular book."[8]

Two other points need to be made about the humanness of James's text. The first has to do with his interest in, and honesty about, the kinds of problems underlying his various theoretical discussions. James took as the problematic of his text the dilemmas posed by the cultural collapse of the post–Civil War era. Simply put, that collapse was what his book was about. Better, put, he took science and philosophy and turned them to the service of the human questions raised by a readership caught in the grip of the cultural collapse: how to get out of a spellbinding morbid mindedness caused by the recognition that to be an American was not to be particularly well founded; how to regain a sense of purpose and vitality and identity when these had all been drained of their myth; how to restore control and individuality in an incorporating, deterministic age.

When James offered a cure for these problems, which was the purpose of the text, he did so without skirting them. That was why, for example, he tried to build a psychology without a soul, because the notion of such a thing had been seen through. And that was why he offered what he called only a theatre of possibilities, because he took seriously the recognition that all human action might be no more than theatrics, but at the same time he saw that what people wanted, at bottom, was a way to understand their several acts as grounded in some kind of hope.

The second point that needs to be made about the humanness of James's text has to do with a limitation, namely, that the text is not about humans in general but about individual humans—that is, humans construed in the manner of James's middle class. James obeyed the canons laid down by his culture when he designed his text: that the subject matter of psychology was the solitary self and not a collective or a group; that the cues to psychological truth were to be found first and foremost within the personal stream of thought; that the way to provide a useful description of the self was to take biographical narrative and raise it to the level of general fact. Portraiture, in a word, was the expected mode of psychological explanation. That James dutifully offered his psychology as a portrait was part of what made his book so accessible and understandable to its readers and reviewers.

If the *Principles of Psychology* provided a portrait, however, it was one that was thoroughly re-visioned—not the usual image of a grounded and integral self but rather an array of images held together without recourse to any foundations and by what was often quite literally sheer dint of will. There was little in James's text of what George Santayana called the "architectonic instinct,"[9] the view that everything could be bound up symmetrically, be presented as in balance, and fit with perfect precision. To be sure, there was a plan to the *Principles*. The text fell very naturally into three major sections, each with a bird's-eye view of the self.[10] And the overall portrait that was provided included most of the classical psychological faculties and features. But the features were not always in their proper place. And their depictions seemed fragmented and splintered. The organization of the portrait, far from precluding discontinuities and interruptions, put them front and center.

These discontinuities and interruptions in the *Principles* are apparent both when the text is viewed overall and when it is examined with an eye on one or another of its individual parts. From the longer point of view, the image of the self that James provided was like a collage: the various chapters hung together more like pictures at an exhibition than as parts of a single, simple description. "The stream of thought is like a river," James wrote in his chapter "Attention," and this river provided the continuity from point to point in his psychological depiction. "But at intervals an obstruction, a set-back, a log-jam occurs, stops the current, creates an eddy, and makes things temporarily move the other way."[11] There was, for James, no way of skipping over these breaks and disruptions, nor could bridges be built to cross over them. Where cracks and crevices in the self were found, they had to be accepted. The self overall was split, or at least split as often as it ever was whole.

The same sense of discontinuity is apparent on the shorter view, for within each chapter that portion of the self-image that was under scrutiny was almost always interrupted, disjointed as well as jointed. James worked the details of his subject matter like a pointilist painter: whatever degree of "generic unity" may have appeared was also almost always conditioned by and coexistent with an equally apparent "generic difference." The individual was not just one self but many. There was no longer just a single agent. To be sure, there were areas of connectedness and unbrokenness; but James put them in their place: "And this unbrokenness in the stream of selves, like the unbrokenness in an exhibition of dissolving views, in no wise implies any farther unity or contradicts any account of plurality in other respects."[12]

The deference that James showed to the dissolving views, and the relative indifference that he often seemed to display toward notions of overarching unity, were largely a result of his perspective and method of investigation. He professed to be a naturalist, and to take a natural-science perspective in the *Principles*.[13] What this amounted to in practice was what James called a kind of common sense approach and appraisal: common sense because it worked with experience as it was concretely given, and because to take everything literally (which is what James did) was the common consensus about how one should live one's life.

Adherence to the dictates of common sense in turn forced a departure from the then-established method of psychological portraiture: to begin with the "mind" as a manifold of ideas and then proceed to break down the manifold into its elementary ideas and build those ideas back up systematically. James started with states of consciousness, "a single pulse of subjectivity, a single psychosis, feeling, or state of mind." Common sense, he argued, finds little warrant for beginning with a "manifold of existing ideas, the notion of such a thing is a chimera."[14] In turn, the end of James's analysis refused what he saw as the siren song of an ideally ordered self, the craving for a unified image. Psychology, James said over and again, is "a mere natural science."

> It is of course conceivable (though far from clearly so) that in the last metaphysical resort all these streams of thought may be thought by one universal All-thinker. But in this metaphysical notion there is no profit for psychology. The idea of Him seems even to exert a positively paralyzing effect on the mind. The existence of finite thoughts is suppressed altogether.[15]

Respect for the nonfoundational, anti-idealist base of psychological experience had as its concomitant an avowal of the physiological rooting of mental activity. The psychologist, James thought, must adopt an almost primitivist posture with regard to his or her subject matter, must assume at the very minimum a strict correlation between the self's "animal" and "rational" natures. James's working hypothesis going into the investigation was "that mental action may be uniformly and absolutely a function of brain-action."[16] What this meant, significantly, was that psychology would have to make do with a mechanistic model of the self, for that was what "brain-action" amounted to when stripped of its romantic and idealist interpretations.

Thus, the initial form and the primary stock of images for James's self-portrait were mechanical in nature: the brain was "like the great commuting switchboard of a central telephone station"; habit was the "enormous flywheel of society"; the self was a series of mutually adapted parts, a bundle of inflowing and outgoing currents passing though a more or less plastic medium. Of course, there may have been things to be said about the self other than what mechanical imagery could convey. But common sense, and again honesty to the perceptions of the everyday person, dictated that these other things could emerge only by working through the mechanical images, and not by working around them.[17]

When James began his text, then, he did so by placing himself and his readers within the familiar if uncomfortable confines of a finite and almost automatic world. "Psychology is the Science of Mental Life," James wrote in his opening sentence, but then immediately deconstructed the statement by adding that it was a science "both of its phenomena and of their conditions."[18] This set the frame for the text, and for the portrait that would follow. What his psychology could explain was "the mind of distinct individuals inhabiting definite portions of a real space and a real time." Included as a necessary part of the portrait was a review of the manner in which the self undergoes, as James put it, the natural conditions of life.[19]

In other words, James's framework precluded the use of what were then the two traditional models of the self. The first was that of the spiritual self, the characterization that posited at the center of the self an "absolute god-given soul" with a set of attendants or faculties. For James, such monarchical images lacked explanatory power: although there was a "great drift of reasons, positive and negative, towing us in their direction,"[20] they could hardly account for the self in the midst of the everyday. Using the faculty of memory as an example of the pitfalls of the spiritualist representation, James asked why the soul should remember so selectively, sometimes forgetting this or that and then sometimes recalling it. And why should illnesses and exhaustion make it so feeble? "Such peculiarities seem quite fantastic, and might, for aught we can see *a priori* be the precise opposites of what they are."[21]

The second established model was that proposed by the associationists. Here the self was constituted by a series of ideas or feelings;

self-identity was explained by the identity of the self's recurrent thoughts. To their credit, said James, the associationists had managed to get along without the notion of a soul, and hence had provided a portrait that was less fantastic than that of the spiritualists. But their model failed equally to account for the natural conditions of mental life. Based as it was on a group of ideas, "separate subjective entities that come and go as they please," the associationist portrait floated in midair. It did not explain the antecedents of the train of ideas, "the effects of fever, exhaustion, hypnotism, old age and the like." Neither did it explain that ideas were bound up after the fact, that

> the ideas and feelings, e.g., which these present printed characters excite in the reader's mind not only occasion movements of his eye and nascent movements of articulation in him, but will some day make him speak, or take sides in a discussion, or give advice, or choose a book to read, differently from what would have been the case had they never impressed his retina.[22]

With the disavowal of the spiritualists and the associationists, James's introductory remarks were done. He had built the frame for his own constructive portrait. He had settled the perspective by which he would make his redescription. Again, the self that he would describe would be created in line with the perceptions of his readers, and on their suspicions about the determinism and lack of solid groundings in their lives. James set the task of psychology in a different direction than the heretofore standard models had done. He gave it a nonfoundational base. He would have to show how genuine human life could be re-created out of natural physiological processes.

James's disposal of the traditional self-portraits also functioned to clear the canvas of his text for his own initial image. "Suppose now that we have a baby before us," James began, "who sees a candle-flame for the first time, and, by virtue of a reflex tendency common in babies of a certain age, extends his hand to grasp it, so that his fingers get burned."[23] James appended two sketches of his nascent image as complements to his written description: there was the head and hand and candle flame, all of which were overlaid with a complex of connecting lines portraying the train of incoming and outgoing currents and their whistle-stops in the eye and hand and brain.

As the image developed, and James worked with it throughout the opening section of the *Principles*, its differences from the traditional models became more distinct. He began with an image that was fundamentally engaged. The picture was of a process in a relational field. There was a baby only as there were the dynamics of seeing and extending and then getting burned. Indeed, the self as James portrayed it was engaged to the point of being determined. Whatever power and dynamics there may have been belonged to the lines and currents; the baby brought "no new elementary form of movement with it" to the process.[24]

By the time the image was exhausted, James had left the reader with a description of physiological reflex arcs, little more than a mechanical drawing. To be sure, the self as James had defined it could function quite well, and as a creature of habit could survive and possibly thrive. But there was no clear autonomy to the self as it had been depicted; while it showed signs of admirable behavior, it could not really be said to act. James let the images run out into a series of questions. Was there any way to talk of this image as having a recognizable personality, or was the self no better than a "hemisphereless animal, who moves in a world of bodies which are all of equal value for him?"[25] Was the picutre of the baby before the candle flame only a polite way of describing what was at bottom an automaton? James's discussion, of course, seemed to suggest that the mechanistic conclusions were almost sufficient to explain his image.

"Almost," however, was a word of some importance when used by James. Thus, at the conclusion of the opening section he softened somewhat the severity of his initial image. Just as he was unwilling to consent to the traditional portraits drawn by the spiritualists and associationists, so he would not "be radical" with his conclusions and join ranks with the Darwinists and the automatists. Automatism was an impossible project, James stated, as much as anything because it could not be carried out without lapsing into the language of human spontaneity: "We talk, when we are darwinizing, as if the mere body that owns the brain had interests. We forget that in the absence of some such superadded commenting intelligence (whether it be that of the animal itself, or only ours or

Mr. Darwin's) the reactions cannot be properly talked of as 'useful' or 'hurtful' at all."[26]

Given the inconclusiveness and even impossibility of carrying out a completely automatist portrait, James found it to be an "unwarranted impertinence," an interpretation that could offer only arbitrary reasons why "under these circumstances, we should be asked to forswear the language of our childhood."[27] This childhood language, of course, was the language of common sense, which spoke of the self as a selecting entity, an agent who had considerations, created and sustained interests, and worked to make real ends appear. It was much better, said James, and equally plausible, to hold to common sense and the narrative that, at least as a conscious being, the self might be efficacious. We might, in making such a narrative, lose something by way of scientific accuracy. But we stood to gain a hypothetical self that met the demands of our practical and aesthetic needs. Who, after all, could consent to the possibility that "we might exhaustively write the biography of those two-hundred pounds, more or less, of warmish albuminoid matter called Martin Luther, without ever implying that it felt"?[28]

And so there might be, finally, a baby before the candle flame as well as a network of currents. The moral of this opening image was that, even when the self was depicted from the strictest standpoint of physical laws and structures, there was no reason why we could not continue to tell a story of human agency. To be sure, this portrait of the self might not suggest the desired realm of absolute spontaneity. "The feelings can produce nothing absolutely new, they can only reinforce and inhibit reflex currents which already exist."[29] And the story of common sense had been chastened, turned from the indicative to the subjunctive. But the image did allow for a possible center of self-determining power, and for some semblance of control over the arbitrary forces of mechanical action.

In the second section of the *Principles*, James turned toward testing his hypothesis about the conscious self and examining the inner world of conscious states (the stream of consciousness and the consciousness of self). His purpose was not to advance an alternative to the image he had just drawn, but to enlarge and develop further that original image by defining the mental actions that corresponded to brain actions. Some alterations in the initial image would have to be made, primarily because the image of the self in a nascent state could not portray the wealth and complexity of human experience. What was required was a picture of the self in a more "mature age," where selection, consideration, and permanent interest held more sway. But all that was in the initial image would remain: the physiological base of all mental activity; the framework of mechanical laws; a sense of reactive spontaneity.

James's procedure in defining this more mature self was precisely the reverse of his initial procedure. In the opening section he began with a very recognizable human form, and then delimited and reduced it to mechanical reflexes until the human form seemed almost entirely superfluous. Here, however, James started with the bare fact of thinking, devoid of all warmth and intimacy, as impersonal as he could make it: "If we could say in English 'it thinks,' as we say 'it rains' or 'it blows,' we should be stating the fact most simply and with the minimum of assumption. As we cannot, we must simply says that thought goes on."[30]

But to say this immediately raised two questions: How is it that thought *goes on* (in what ways can the dynamism and activity of thought be described)? And second, what is this *thought* that goes on; where is the element of permanency, or at least of continuity, that allows us to talk of thought at all? James answered the first question abruptly: to say that thought goes on was to say that it was in flux, was something in which "no state once gone can recur and be identical with what it was before." We may well get the same object of thought twice over. But the thought of an object and the thought-again of the same object were vastly different.[31]

The image of thought as a flux was, however, less than precise, for while thought might be ever-changing, and never identically recurring, it did have a felt sense of unity (or at least of continuity). Consciousness was never simply chopped up; common sense held, and on good introspective grounds, that thought also was something that could be said to flow. To be sure, the substantive parts of thought (for example, the subject or topics of a sentence) did indeed seem separate, and if that were all there was to be accounted for, then clearly there would be no sense at all in talking about continuity. But if we drew out the whole of a thought—the verbs, prepositions, and qualifiers, the gaps and feelings of absence—if, in a word, we reinstated "the vague to its proper place in our mental life," then we had to describe the continuity supposed by common sense. "A river or stream are the metaphors by which it is most naturally described." Thought meant both the "pailsful" and "quartpotsful" of the stream, and the "free water of consciousness" surrounding them.[32]

It should be noted in passing that this sketch of consciousness as a stream of thought always flowing on placed James once again in opposition to the then-reigning descriptions of mental activity. In those, thought was conceived as a train of ideas: continuity was posited in the recurring ideas or cars of the train; change had to do with the train overall, the fact that it was jointed at best, with irreducible gaps (absences of feeling rather than feelings of absence) between one car and the next. In James's text continuity was located in the flow of the stream. We got a sense of change because we found that we could not step into the same stream twice.

There was more, of course, to the stream than just the fact of its never recurring. At a minimum, each thought appeared with a sense of ownership: "It seems as if the elementary psychic fact were not thought or this thought or that thought but my thought, every thought being owned." To draw the stream of thought was thus to draw it as a personal stream. The stream as such was an abstraction. An adequate description had to portray consciousness as it was given, namely, as delimited and defined by personal interests, selections, and, at a "higher" level, by aesthetic and practical demands. James wrote:

> Out of what is in itself an indistinguishable, swarming continuum, devoid of distinction or emphasis, our senses make for us, by attending to this notion and ignoring that, a world full of contrasts, of sharp accents. . . . And then again, among the sensations we get from separate things, what happens? The mind selects again. It chooses certain of the sensations to represent the thing most truly, and considers the rest as its appearances, modified by the conditions of the moment.[33]

And as the stream of thought appeared always as a personal stream, so could it be said that the conscious flow was but another name for personality. Or rather, what in effect was meant by personality was no more nor less than the states of mind viewed as interested, attended to, and selected. The stream of thought was the original of all our ideas about personality; there were no "marks of personality to be gathered aliunde." As James said, "no psychology, at any rate, can question the existence of personal selves. The worst a psychology can do is so to interpret the nature of these selves as to rob them of their worth."[34]

By the end of the chapter on the stream of consciousness, the bare notion of thought had given way to a description of an active and, at the very least, a semiautonomous personality. All of this had emerged, moreover, without violating the principles of the initial image: James had only added details. The effect of this detail work, however, was to change the entire emphasis of the picture of the self. Where before there was only a secondary and inconsequential sense of personal efficacy, now there emerged a self gaining possession of its inner world, steering its course through a river of almost limitless possibilities. Self-control had been enlarged to include ownership and constructive capability; the self now acted creatively, "very much as a sculptor works on his block of stone." One could, of course, turn all of this back "to that black and jointless continuity of space and moving clouds of swarming atoms which science calls the only real world." But at the same time, "the world we feel and live in will be that which our ancestors and we, by slowly cumulative strokes of choice, have extricated out of this."[35]

What James had not yet accounted for was the sense of conscious identity, who exactly it was that lived and felt and acted "by slowly cumulative strokes." Personality, after all, does not by itself give us a person; and although personality was certainly represented in the image of the stream of thought, it was unclear whether the image was adequate to represent a full-fledged person. James's language, moreover, with all the talk about actors, sculptors, and so forth, had seemed to suggest that a substantial self operated on the stream. All of which raised the question of whether a second image of the self as a spiritual being was needed in addition to that of the stream of thought.

James's approach to the notion of self-consciousness, and the way in which he avoided the conclusions of the spiritualists, was to ask what, in common sense terms, was meant by the self: what was the content of our division of the world into "me" and "not me"; what was meant by our talk of an identifying agent or "I"? Taking the points in order, James first explained that the "empirical Self is the sum total of all that he CAN call his." It included a person's material, social, and spiritual dimensions, everything in which a person could legitimately claim to have an interest. In fact, of course, human interests were variable, and when, over time, we spoke about who we were, we usually referred not to a permanent but to a "fluctuating material."[36] When wrapped in thought, for instance, we might disregard our bodies and consider them as having nothing to do with ourselves. At the point of death, however, the body may assume almost the whole of our interest and thus of our sense of ourselves. The same vacillation was true with regard to our acts, which came and went, assumed greater or lesser importance and memorableness from one time to another.

The empirical self, then, was nothing more than the stream of thought in its characteristic form of being owned and being interested. There was no need to go beyond the image of the stream of thought when depicting the "me" and "not me": the fluidity of the image provided an adequate representation of the self as a "loosely construed thing," while the stability of the image gave an adequate portrayal of the defining acts of self-reference, and without allowing them to be taken as definite, immutable facts. The consciousness of an objective self was simply a further, more precise way of describing the dynamic activity of the stream of thought. It was the final word needed to explain how the stream flowed; it was "as strong an example as there is of that selective industry of the mind."[37]

As was the case with the notion of the empirical self (me), so it was the idea of the self-identifying agent (I). What, at least for common sense, the word *I* meant was simply a felt center of interest: thought seemed to imply a thinker of some sort, a focus of accretion and appropriation, a "real belonging, to a real Owner." Most of this feeling of a center could be explained in terms of bodily processes and reactions, cephalic adjustments, and the like. But there was also something of a conscious concomitant to these movements, which was best described as a kind of welcoming or rejecting of possible facts.[38]

All of this, again, was only a restatement of what was given in the image of the stream of thought. There was always some passing thought in the stream that was central or present before all others, but which, because it was distinct but not separate from the thoughts before and after it, could also be said to be appropriative of them: "This is what collects,—'owns' some of the past facts which it surveys, and disowns the rest,—and so makes a unity that is actualized and anchored and does not merely float in the blue air of possibility."[39]

There was thus no need to introduce a second image to account for personal identity. If anything, the stream of thought showed that "the Soul truly explained nothing; the syntheses, which she performed, were simply taken ready-made and clapped on to her as expressions of her nature taken after the fact." And the image of the stream preserved what was of value in the spiritualist theory (and what, according to James, was lost in the extension of that theory into a pure ego), namely, an image of a self with "some semblance of nobility of outlook. She was called active; might select; was responsible, and permanent in her way."[40]

With these remarks James's second image of the self was complete: corresponding to the world of mechanical and fixed processes was a cumulative and constructive center of personal responsibility. The self as James had portrayed it had once again the status of a real actor capable of constructing a life while remaining open to new constructions, to what amounted to changes of mind. Above all, it was a self with real decision-making power, still within a mechanistic order but no longer determined by it. Each of us, James wrote, "chooses, by his ways of attending to things, what sort of a universe he shall appear to himself to inhabit. So the seeker of his truest, strongest, deepest self must review the list carefully, and pick out the one on which to stake his salvation. Once more, then, our self-feeling is in our power."[41]

What remained in the balance at the close of this second section was the authenticity of the self-definition and of the constructed world, the questions of reality, illusion, and truth. The images of the self that James had given thus far did not account for the genuineness of self-activity in a world outside the mind; that would have to wait for the final expansion of the image in the third section of the *Principles*. But feelings of reality, if not yet the reality of those feelings, had been established: that was what the image of the stream of thought was intended to do. And if it did not yet recover the authenticity of the self's activity, it did recover the notion of dramatic activity, the idea that in "the theatre of simultaneous possibilities" a performance was going on, and that "in it things are really being decided from one moment to another, and that it is not the dull rattling off of a chain that was forged innumerable ages ago. This appearance, which makes life and history tingle with such a tragic zest, *may* not be an illusion."[42]

"After inner perception, outer perception," James opened his third and final section of the *Principles*, and his turnabout was as unexpected as it was abrupt.[43] What, after all, should have come next, and particularly as James now had to deal with questions of reality and authenticity, was a discussion of the permanence and being of the self, some sort of argument that could clinch the image from above. What James did, however, was to return to the primary and sensory field of the initial section of the text: the final depiction would be that of a reflex arc, now a tripartite image of sensory input, central reasoning, and motor output. As the conscious self arose from a nonfoundational world, so it now had to plunge back into that world "as bridges plunge their piers into the rock."[44] Whatever sense of authenticity was to be had would have to be had on that basis.

There was, however, something new in this return: James added a background image to the primary processes; he replaced the self not just back into its nascent state but into a social world. Or rather, he replaced the self back into a socially unstable world, a world without boundaries, in which there was no order save that of a Darwinian competition. Prior to this the self had been depicted as alone, but that, James knew, was an abstraction. From here on the self would be set in the world where James's readers lived, where all sorts of selves were at work, and where all of those selves were equally interested—and interested in themselves.

Thus the theater of possibilities was given character. It now became what amounted to a "gory cradle" and theater of war. And the self was given a character as well. Acting as it had to in a world struggling for survival, it was depicted as a fighter. Again, in the first two sections James's images were portrayed without a background, and thus as relatively innocent: the example of the baby before the candle flame demonstrated at worst an impersonal, mechanistic process; the conscious self, with its selections, interests, and considerations, was simply selectively interested. Here, however, all that the self was and had was recast, placed in a combative stance. Mental functions became "weapons of the mind." Ideas were judged for their capacity to "draw blood." Self-power became the hero's ability to stand his ground in a world of strenuous struggle and effort.[45]

With this background drawn, James began to set out his final image of the self. His first step was to remind the reader what this return to the primary processes meant. After all of the discussion of consciousness, James explained, it was necessary to remember just how small was the arsenal of the self's creative and original forces, and how much of the self was mechanistically determined in advance: "The whole neural organism, it will be remembered, is, physiologically considered, but a machine for converting stimuli into reactions, and the intellectual part of our life is knit up with but the middle or 'central' part of the machine's operations." Even this statement could be misleading, for not all intellectual activity was genuinely productive. Most thinking was "only reproductive." Only "the ability to deal with NOVEL data" could be called truly productive.[46]

Actually, this was more than a reminder, for it led James to delete much of what were then supposed to be original elements of the self's conscious activity. On the near side of consciousness—on the side of sensation—human imagination and the perception of space and of things could all be reduced to fixed and native operations of the reflex machine: they were conditioned rather than conditioning functions of the self. On the far side of consciousness, most of the self's productive output could be ascribed to automatic causes: instincts were not "prophetic powers" but simply "functional correlatives of [a reflex] structure"; emotions were not originators of bodily action but only the action itself.[47]

The quantitative adjustment of the self-portrait served James in two ways. First, it restored the proper balance to the portrait overall: the cumulative strokes of self-definition took up but a small portion of the canvas; most of what appeared when the self was described was, again, pulled from the stock of mechanical and material images. Also, however, and more important for James's purposes here, it provided him a chance to show what a marvelously functioning entity the physiological self was, and indeed what an ally this entity could be in the struggle for survival. Here, after all, was a being with its own dynamics and powers, capable of fighting its own battles and standing its ground in a world of competition. Here was an army of primary processes already made, ready to deal with the major adaptive functions of life, made to do the groundwork of living. According to James there was no better or richer example of an adaptive mechanism to be found in the natural realm.

And with the army of primary resources taking care, almost automatically, of adaptation, the conscious self was now freed to attend to the tasks of variation, the creating and sustaining of the new. Conscious production had nothing to do with the basic tasks of life, the need to make a living and such: the "machinery" had already taken care of that. Rather, it had to do with the power to manage and to transform the primary processes, to desire, propose, and redirect the mechanical input and output of the self. All of this was, again, but an expansion of the image of the self that had been given up to this point. James did not have to add anything new. He had simply pointed out another dimension of the self that had not been clear before.

Precisely what, according to James, this transforming power of consciousness amounted to was the positing and sustaining of an ideal or essential world. Simply stated, it was the effort to turn the subjunctive possibilities brought to consciousness into indicatives and imperatives. It was not the recovery of some truth or pure form: as James explained, "There is no property ABSOLUTELY essential to any one thing." And because it had not the guarantee of an absolute realm, indeed because it always stood confronting other possible worlds and essences, it was always a risky business and an effort, a "pure inward willingness" to stake a claim on an uncertain ground.[48] But this was an immensely important task, and more than that, it was as much as anyone could ask for, for it gave the self a chance to be a hero.

For the sake of a more adequate description, James divided this transforming power of consciousness into two functions: the capacity of the self to cognize reality—that is, to establish a world of ultimate beliefs and concerns—and the ability of the self to turn to "this world which it has made, act on the world of its making with a Will." Strictly speaking, these two ways of constructing a world and acting upon it were but two perspectives on the same psychological fact. "Will and belief, in short, meaning a certain relation between objects and the Self, are two names for one and the same

PSYCHOLOGICAL phenomenon."[49] Belief was the phenomenon viewed from the side of sensory input; it was the claim of consciousness that certain facts were or were not ultimately significant. Volition was the same phenomenon seen from the side of motor output; it concerned the "conscious comment" that certain facts were to be held as ultimate ends and thus as springs of action.

Both belief and action had a general and a specific meaning, depending on the level of conscious effort needed to maintain a stable relationship between the self and the particular state of mind. Some facts came to us as "stinging events," with an indisputable claim to being real; any such input, as well as any input that was not contradicted, was simply accepted as real. In these cases belief was only another, slightly stronger expression of the fact of human attention, an explanation of the "psychic attitude" toward the selected portions of the conscious stream. So was volition generally the acceptance of certain ideas as "urgent" and compelling; it was the agreement to accept these ideas as the "prime conditions of impulsive power."[50] In these cases it was difficult to distinguish volition from simple ideomotor and reflex action.

Rarely, however, did the self find itself in an easygoing world of stinging events and urgent impulses. Inputs seldom "fill the mind solidly to the exclusion of contradictory ideas." Impulses, in part because the neural machinery was so complex, most times ran at variance to one another, and were either explosive or obstructed. And adding to the conflict was the fact that consciousness always had a say in the relationships to be established. "The whole distinction of real and unreal is thus grounded on two mental facts,—first, that we are liable to think differently of the same, and second, that when we have done so, we can choose which way of thinking to adhere to and which to disregard."[51] In these situations of competition and contradiction, belief and will came fully into play, giving solidity to the worlds of facts that had been selected.

In its full application, then, belief was not merely attention but an active assertion, a wager that this or that fact was real, despite the counterclaims that were always rearing their heads. Likewise, volition was an effort, a fiat or resolve made "in the line of greatest resistance; it was the establishment of dominance, the sustaining of urgency for the sake of action." "The strong-willed man," James explained, "is the man who hears the still small voice unflinchingly

. . . who looks at its face, consents to its presence, clings to it, affirms it, and holds it fast, in spite of the host of exciting mental images which rise in revolt against it and would expel it from the mind."[52]

"Sow an action, reap a habit," James wrote in the margin of his copy of the *Principles*, and he went on to add: "Sow a habit, reap a character. Sow a character, reap a destiny."[53] What emerged from James's description of belief and will, and more generally from his overall depiction of the self in the third section, was an image of the self with a full power of definition, a capacity both to legislate over experience and to mold and recreate it in a fixed destiny. In turn, the questions of the reality of the self had been answered. As James put it, "[T]he *fons* and *origo* of all reality, whether from the absolute or the practical point of view, is thus subjective, is ourselves." Concomitantly, human interests and aspirations were congenial with, and more than that constitutive of, the ultimate and authentic nature of things. Wants, desires, and demands were now the "ultimate fixities from which . . . the whole chain of our beliefs depends, object hanging to object, as the bees, in swarming, hang to each other until *de proche en proche*, the supporting branch, the Self, is reached and held."[54]

Finally, all this depiction of ultimacy was also a description of the religious dimension of life: the Jamesian self had not only a power of definition but what amounted to a power of conversion. Belief, according to James, was, in the last resort, a conversion of facts into "settled creeds";[55] it was the assertion not only of a moral but also of a religious way and rule of life. And to turn with the will toward a possible world of experience was to create a religious experience; it was a fiat or resolve to live life in obedience to a world of orienting centers. To be sure, the absolute center of orientation was the self. But belief involved a fully religious experience nonetheless.

And so there was, finally, not just an original but an ultimate contribution that the human could make to life: as the reactive spontaneity of James's first image gave way to autonomy and some sense of creative control, so now it was expanded once again to include the assertion of an underived conscious effort. James's initial hypothesis—that consciousness was "an organ added for the sake of steering a nervous system"—had borne itself out and then some. The pilot had not only regained control but had become a commander capable of ordering and, if need be, reordering the course of life. Everything hinged on effort.

Lest we go beyond James in the assessment of his final image, we need to recall that the primary functions of the self remained in force; consciousness did not present anything new or create out of nothing. The conscious self depended on its physiological base; its creative efforts were always variations, realizations of possibilities already given. But though the organ of consciousness needed the mechanism of the neural system as its base, it was no longer caught in its physiological web. The conscious comment was secondary but had all the priority; the neural machine needed consciousness to give it existence, and "[backed] us up instantaneously" when consciousness made its demands. Returning to the image of the theater of possibilities, James concluded that "the psychic side of the phenomenon thus seems, somewhat like the applause or hissing at a spectacle, to be an encouraging or adverse comment on what the machinery brings forth." But in doing this "she figures not as an epiphenomenon" but as a formative factor of the mechanical acts, "a co-determinant of their mechanical effectiveness."[56]

In an 1882 article entitled "Rationality, Activity, and Faith," James gave a summary statement of his point of view about psychology. An enduring and successful portrait of human life, he wrote, "must not be one that baffles and disappoints our dearest desires and most cherished powers." Ultimate principles should not be presented as incommensurate with human capabilities. What was at all times required was a proclamation, in one form or another, that the nature of things was compatible with the things of human nature. Such a message had been transmitted in all great periods of revival and renewal: "What were Luther's mission and Wesley's but appeals to powers which even the meanest of men might carry with them. . . . How did Kant and Fichte, Goethe and Schiller, inspire their time with cheer, except by saying 'Use all your powers; that is the only obedience which the Universe exacts.'"[57]

It would be possible to conclude here with James's own assessment of his effort in his text; that he had tried to provide (and, we can add, succeeded in providing) a contemporary translation of the prophetic call to human empowerment; that he had offered a redescription of the self in which a vital life could be led without recourse to some higher realm. And that conclusion would fit, because this is in fact what James accomplished in the *Principles*. But it would not fit in other ways. It does not address the limitations of the text. It leaves James more innocent than he was in the design of his redescription. Finally, this was not James's only conclusion about his psychology. Later he would begin to re-vision the self again on the conviction that the revival in the *Principles* had been headed the wrong way.

To begin to understand the limitations of the *Principles*, we need to return briefly to the disease of the self as James, and his middle-class culture, defined it: morbid self-consciousness born of a perception of the contingency of life, a failure at the level of self-feeling and self-esteem. What James grappled with was a tragedy of power that had been broken. The story as he told it was one of ruptured links between vision and action, of dead-beating impulses and aspirations, of a self that "never gets its voice out of the minor into the major key, or its speech out of the subjunctive into the imperative mood, never breaks the spell, never takes the helm into its hands."[58] The human drama, to borrow from James's stock of images, had become like a performance of *Hamlet* without its star performer. The script remained as it was written, the central part there for the taking, but no actor to play the role, or if there was, he or she stood stagestruck before the theater, filled with the inward hollowness of forgotten lines.[59]

The problem with James's interpretation was not that it was inaccurate, nor that the situation he defined was anything less than genuine, and a crisis of some proportion. Rather, it was that James never looked beyond the problem to see its other side. Quite simply, he failed to recall that the drama of *Hamlet* was a tragedy played *with* as well as *without* its star performer, and more generally that actors are figures in dramas and only by an act of forgetting think that they make the dramas up. As a result of this partial vision, when it came time to fill the void with his regenerated images James did so without even a glance at the problems that might ensue, the dilemmas posed by human power once again unleashed. There was a naiveté about James's image, an assumption that self-assertion and dominance, the right to believe as one will, were antidotes to determinism rather than expressions of it.

These problems were exacerbated by the fact that the portrait in the *Principles* had few bonds of sympathy, and hence of responsibility. The Jamesian self floated unfettered by any wider frame of reference or meaning than itself. It was not only isolated for the sake of analysis but isolate, without any sense of connectivity. All of which made practical activity little more than mere activism, a cult of movement for its own sake, a staking of a personal claim whose only watchword could be the exclamation "More!" Life at the helm, where courses of action were being decided, where the zest and sting of life struck against a proud face looking forward: that was the meaning and end of James's self-portrait. It is difficult to see what else it could offer other than a chance for self-aggrandizement.

It may be objected that this assessment stretches James's image beyond where he intended it to go, that his vision, albeit implicit for the most part in the *Principles*, was of a republican ideal, an egalitarian society in which there was a common interest in preserving the rights of all to their private interests. There is merit to this objection, for throughout most of the text no conflict was mentioned, nor did it need to be, between one self-project and another: the drama was all internal. But with the final section of the book, the facade of gentility fell away. Armed now with an array of weapons and poised in a combative stance, the ideal seemed to have taken on another meaning; the republican self asserting its legitimate rights had become the imperial self legitimating, on the grounds of self-interest and the necessity of success, its right to conquest and unlimited expansion.

A better objection would be that James did not altogether realize what he had envisioned in his text; his stock of images blinded him. And in turn he remained blind to the outcome of his vision: it would take the success of his image during the late nineteenth century to bring the problems home. Now, what James envisioned was a self determined by a free flow of forces, without any deeper grounding than a contingent and random variation. But because he used the images of machines—dead things without any integrity or life of their own—to explain literally what this free flow was all about, he thought that freedom, like all machines, was something that could be controlled. Thus he gave out one of the most dangerous prescriptions one can give to a person or a society in the midst of depression and collapse: Take charge of your freedom, it's there for the taking; take control of your dramas, make them your own. This prescription is dangerous because it sends the person into a mania: My effort is my only chance! The result is what James got back in the decades after the publication of the *Principles*: people continuing to deny contingency and freedom, people asserting, like the actor who identifies too closely with a role, that life is a script of which "I" am the author, something that can be put to work "for me."

As I said before, the *Principles* was not James's last word on the self. While it remained the basic image out of which he worked, James did, in time, work out of it. And to much that I have said here James would assent. As it became evident to him just how his image, and others like his, functioned in society, he began to retrace all of the lines and shapes of the self he had drawn. As the meaning of his book as a cultural phenomenon became clear to him, he returned to it in an effort to give it a broader frame and meaning. The truth of his text, after all, was for James what became of his definitions in outward fact. As he witnessed what happened to them in the cultural revival of America's middle class at the turn of the century, he understood that a different kind of truth and a new set of principles needed to be developed for his portrait of the self.

II

THE LATER YEARS: 1890–1910

3

The Romance of
Self-Assertion

What is good? All that heightens the feeling of power, the will
to power, power itself in man.
What is bad? All that proceeds from weakness.
What is happiness? The feeling that power increases—that a
resistance is overcome.
Not contentment, but more power; not peace at all, but war;
not virtue, but proficiency (virtue in the Renaissance style,
virtu, virtue free of moralic acid).
The weak and ill-constituted shall perish; first principle of our
philanthropy. And one shall help them to do so.
                              Friedrich Nietzsche, *The Anti-Christ*

With the advance of the 1890s into the early 1900s, the Jamesian
self seemed a dream that had come true. Self-realization—the act of
claiming one's freedom—was once more in vogue; the obstructed
American will, steeped in disappointment, vexed, morbid, was suddenly explosive, caught up in and carried forward by a national
crusading impulse. "In our country," wrote a chagrined William
Dean Howells, "where every genuine talent, young as well as old, is
characterized by the instinct if not the reason of reality, nothing of
late has been heard but the din of arms, the horrid tumult of the
swashbuckler swashing on his buckler."[1] Jacob Riis, reporting to
the middle classes as a "war correspondent" on the urban underside
of the spirit of violent adventure, struck the image more precisely:
"The Man with the Knife" was his description of the new American

Adam.[2] Riis left it to his readers to conclude, as they did, that where there was one knife, there had better be two.

Twenty-eight books on Napoleon appeared in the United States between 1894 and 1896. Seventy-one historical orders and patriotic societies started up in the final quarter of the century. It was a time of historical romance, of the aggressive, imperial self. Where problems and weaknesses were perceived, strong new narratives were built over them; the depressed self was hidden behind a facade of military decorations and courtly titles. The Knights of Labor, the Brotherhood of the Kingdom, Knights of Temperance, the Order of the White Rose, Young Crusaders, Knights of King Arthur, the Princely Knights of Character Castle, Colonial Dames, Daughters of the American Revolution: the list went on and on.[3] Human endeavor was stretched to a point of heroic improbability, just far enough to open an escape into a realm where comparisons, criticisms, and criteria could not easily follow.

The spirit of historical romance had been present all along, but until the nineties it could muster neither a strong following nor a clear field upon which to carry out its adventures. Then, and it seemed all at once, came waves of venturesome volunteers, all drawn by a rhetoric of the self's recreative potential, each filled with visions of sacred battles to be fought, new foreign frontiers to be crossed and won. Urban tenements and slum wards suddenly caught the attention of the middle classes; they were redescribed as battlefields, combat zones to be quelled, reformed, pulled back from the brink of certain disaster. Imperialistic adventures and missions overseas were viewed as enticing and exciting. The Atlantic and Pacific oceans were hailed as new frontiers for a country turned in on itself; they could open vistas, "breaking the bond of custom, offering new experience, calling out new institutions and activities."[4]

External quests of expansion and reformation were matched by an internal crusade to reclaim, under the banner of a new science of the mind, the teeming resources of the just-discovered mental realm. "New Thought" became the rallying cry, not just of a religious group but of the whole social movement; it provided the key to unlock the mysterious, magical powers of the self's mental resources.[5] Thought over action, narrative in the place of fact: that was the way to self-fulfillment. As Washington Gladden stated in the opening sentence of *Ruling Ideas of the Present Age*: "The first words of the Forerunner who came preaching in the wilderness of Judea were these: 'Change your minds, for the Kingdom of Heaven is at hand.'"6 Few questioned the accuracy of Gladden's rendering of the text.

The romantic resurgence presented a revitalized image of the self. It is tempting to see it as an image born of confidence, of optimism about the future, and of a belief that the era of self-loss and disintegration had ended.7 To hold with such an assessment, however, would be to forget that the movement was romantic in the first place, indeed, that the swing to romance was a purposeful reaction, *A Lover's Revolt*, as John DeForest called it in his novelistic turn from realism to romanticism.8 It would be to forget as well the element of conscious denial in the agreement, quite open and explicit, that "no one paints life as it is,—thank heaven!—for we could not bear it. Somewhere we must compromise with the dulnesses, the secrecies, the indecencies, the horrors of life."9

To be sure, utterances of confidence abounded; a new world order awaited a new self, if only Americans would create it. But most often the words belied what lay beneath them; their rising tones had more in common with the evening star of Wagner than with Emerson's clear, bright morning star. Rudyard Kipling, recounting the remarks of a Vermont woman who lived across the ridge from him, caught the current of desolation at the core of the optimistic mood: "Be ye the new lights 'crost the valley yonder? Ye don't know what a comfort they've been to me this winter. Ye aren't goin' to shroud 'em up—or be ye?"10

To those who retained a measure of realism, the feeling was that romanticism was being reared not in an era of change, but at the end stage of the earlier cultural collapse; it arose just as the disintegration of the decades following the Civil War had become permanently established. By the 1890s the capitalist and corporate order was firmly consolidated, past the ambiguity of its industrial phase. With the repeal of the Silver Act in 1893—the symbolic final blow to the old industrial order—the consensus was that the age of noncorporate enterprise had ended.11 Social turbulence, too, had solidified into a relatively rigid class structure with limited, predictable, and, above all else, well-controlled avenues of movement. This did, of course, bring a measure of relief to an embattled middle class; yet it also brought a sense of failure. Over and again the complaint was raised that America had succumbed to the fate of the Europeans.[12] The story of the "city upon a hill," there for all the world to see, was, in the end, little better than a twice-told tale of the Old World's woes. Frederick Jackson Turner, speaking from the halls of the White City at the 1893 Columbian Exposition in Chicago, gave official endorsement to the feeling that the present age was an age just ending: "And now, four centuries from the discovery of America, at the end of a hundred years of life under the Constitution, the frontier has gone, and with its going has closed the first period of American history."[13]

Set in the backwater of the *fin de siècle*, or at least in an atmosphere where, as Henry Adams said, "everyone talked, and seemed to feel *fin de siècle*,"[14] the new romanticism was finally little more than a kind of manic response, a movement of self-affirmation based not on renewal but on an aggressive denial of the culture's ills. Rther than work their way through the collapse of self-definitions, Americans simply raised over them a set of clichés that would provide a feeling of self-elation. And with no genuine alternatives available, the manic redescription took the route of high fiction and fantasy. Like James M. Barrie's *Peter Pan*, which was first staged during these years, romanticism afforded an opportunity to denounce the now settled cultural depression by way of make-believe, a flight to a realm where the pains of unwanted maturity did not have to be endured.

The romantic vitality, in turn, was the vitality of a blatant illusion, a regeneration of self-definitions forged by forcing into equal prominence with the facts of a century at its close the unreal image of a dawning new age. "When the life of man becomes a harmony of God," stated George Herron, his words showing clearly the wish to be anywhere but up against the facts, "sickness will be among the old things that have passed away. Implicit obedience to the will of God that was in Christ would abolish disease in three generations."[15] There was the offer of some renewal in a statement such as this. But it is, and was, questionable whether it offered anything more than just a means of diversion, a "museum of idols," "all the things without being the one thing needed."[16]

The manner in which the romantic movement created and sustained its illusion of a regenerated self comes clearer if we examine the various elements that made up its new world order. The first, and because it set the context for the overall pattern of life it was probably the most important, was the image of the self in a state of war, the depiction of the individual caught up in a crusading, militaristic age.[17] During the 1890s the whole notion of war was renovated, cleansed of anything that could give a moment's pause. Whatever memories may have persisted of actual wars were either discarded or denied; the warrior image was sanitized, rid of all its unpalatable contradictions and horrors.

Indicative of this process of purification was the way in which the Civil War was reinterpreted. Statues were raised not as memorials for the war dead but in recognition of the ever-living spirit of conquest and victory. General Sherman became the typical warrior-hero; Lincoln was shorn of his ambivalence and restored to a straight-forward commander in chief. "Through our great good fortune," said Oliver Wendell Holmes, Jr., in a speech commemorating the war (not the Union or the Union cause), "in our youth our hearts were touched with fire. It was given us to learn at the outset that life is a profound and passionate thing."[18] There was little negative comment in Holmes's remembrance; the passion and the profundity had to do only with the exceptional zest of the experience. Whereas so recently the war had been seen as a deadening force, devouring the conqueror along with the conquered, it had now become a form of secular conversion, an unequivocal means whereby individuals could carve out their own destinies, make their marks on life.

"I am for war," wrote the poet Richard Hovey in his 1891 drama *The Marriage of Guenevere*, coining the first phrase of the new romantic creed. He then went on to clarify what he meant, warning against those "men in peace" who, "lacking brave emulation and the zeal of a great cause, fall to their petty ends and, letting their high virtues atrophy, wallow in lust and avarice, till the heart and nobler functions rot away and leave a people like an oyster, all stomach."[19] Hovey's message was carefully drawn: his argument was not with pacifists (crusaders for peace, after all, could be as belligerent as crusaders for war),[20] but with men *in peace*, that is, with the situation in which people placed themselves. His advocacy was simply for the state of war, and not, it should be noted, for any particular cause that would produce the commitment to struggle in its behalf. Causes, of course, remained important: they served as springboards for acts of war, stimulating and refining the martial virtues. But they always had to be subordinated to the actual fact of the fight; they were like passive weights, existing only to provide the feeling of uplift.

Hovey's logic, and the general romantic logic that it mirrored, did make sense. If the romantic illusion was to succeed, it could brook no opposition, especially from within; causes had to be emptied of the ambiguities that inevitably followed in their train. Subordination, of course, was not the only way to achieve this unambiguous end. A method of exaggeration was also employed in which causes were made into *grand* causes (and the grander the better), so sweeping and general that they could not run aground on practical considerations. Justice, the Kingdom of God, the total eradication of disease, pauperism and exorbitant wealth (preferably in one or two generations): such were the kinds of causes, all so broad that they could not raise objections, that filled the sails of the romantic quests. And why not make them broad? Causes, after all, had no limits other than what humans decided: the grander the cause, then, the better.

A similar aggrandizement was performed in the opposite direction, too, in an effort to turn the perceived antagonists and enemies of good into forces much larger than life. The outlook of the romanticists was rife with conspiratorial images and views of history. Infidels and barbarians, robber barons and captains of industry, "mob-rule in the day of wrath": such were the epithets attached to the gathering, threatening forces. "Slow work, yes!" wrote Jacob Riis in his *Battle with the Slum*; "but be it ever so slow, the battle has got to be fought, and fought out. For it is one thing or the other: either wipe out the slum or it wipes us out. Let there be no mistake. It cannot be shirked. Shirking means surrender, and surrender means the end of government by the people."[21]

There was a partial exception to all of this subordination and delimiting of causes: the notions of struggle and conflict, understood as causes, were granted an almost absolute primacy in the romantic valorization of war. Romanticists justified their emphasis on the good of the war state by becoming preachers of struggle in a world of fate. Civilization implied a race to get ahead or be extinguished. Jesus became the great initiator of revolution. Progress and reform hinged for their arrival and success on the prime moving cause of conflict. The only fact was force, or so it was argued; force, above all else, was irresistible and unchangeable. The cause of conflict stood, in essence, as the one idea worth fighting for, the notion upon which people could justifiably stake their aggressive claims.[22] If the reasoning here was circular, that was scarcely noticed, and when it was, it was seen as a circle of vast scope, a mirror of the ground of life.

One hundred years earlier the prevailing word about assertion had been, as Alexander Hamilton put it in a note published in the *New York Pamphlet* and other papers, that "it seems to have been reserved to the people of this country, to decide by their conduct and example, the important question, whether societies of men are really capable or not, of establishing good government from reflection and choice, or whether they are forever destined to depend, for their political constitutions on accident and force."[23] By the 1890s, however, that understanding had been altered, if not also reversed. Under the sway of evolutionary schemes that gained impetus from a notion of crisis and conflict, accident and force were merged with reflection and choice to create what Oliver Wendell Holmes, Jr., called a "new path" of societal movement and law. "The conception of law" that Holmes stood for, he explained, "is that the law is the expression, more or less deflected by opposition, of the dominant force in society. . . . People want to know under what circumstances and how far they will run the risk of coming against what is so much stronger than themselves."[24]

Holmes's statement was more extreme and positivistic than most; his conception left little room for reflections of eternal governing purposes and principles. Others, not willing to state the case that baldly, put it somewhat more softly: they blended force with the notion of ideals; the struggle was that of the inbreaking new world order. However stated, the point remained the same: the logic of force served to legitimate the use of force and the valorization of war. "The work of missions is not a wrecking expedition but a war of conquest," said William Ashmore in a speech before the Student Volunteer Movement for Foreign Missions.[25] There was no need for any further justification. To show that the struggle was for the sake of the struggle was somehow to put people's minds at rest.

What was gained in all of this romantic reaffirmation of war was a break in the siege mentality of the post–Civil War decades, a renewed sense of life and of the self as productive and engaged. The struggle, even when it issued in little more than fantasies of aggression, offered a way out of morbid self-consciousness. And the advancement and valorization of activism, fueled by an apocalyptic imagery of great evils and even greater goods, did provide a feeling of self-transcendence.

And yet what was missing in this resurgence of the warrior mentality was any recognition of the reality of struggle, the dimensions of failure, tragedy, and suffering. War, according to the romantic model, was more like a sport than anything else, a wager with hardly any risk at all. Critics with an interest not so much in the exercise as in the outcome of the proposed conflicts complained that the romantic model failed to consider the intricacies and difficulties of their ventures, not to mention the inevitable betrayals, horrors, and compromises. "Those who study pages written in blood," said the Congregational minister Amory Bradford, "not unnaturally feel that they know some elements in the problems that never reached pulpits and professor's chairs. They are right. These men are not all dreamers and imposters."[26] Criticisms such as this from below were joined by questions from within and above the movement. As William Dean Howells wrote: "I find duels and battles set forth as the great and prevalent human events; I find pride and revenge worshipped as right and fine, but no suggestion of the shame and heartache which have followed the doers of violence in all times."[27]

Perhaps the most telling critical comment, however, came from a most unlikely source, Andrew Carnegie, who concluded his examination of the new world of social conflict that was then being promoted by saying: "This is not evolution, but revolution."[28] Carnegie took the popular idealization of the destructive element to its logical conclusion: assuming that the call to arms was more than a mere rhetorical device, he asked, was it not seeking to "overturn present conditions," and would it not lead to a complete rupture with and uprooting of things as they were at the present time? Carnegie baited his readers by confronting them with the results of their proposed adventures; he caught them at their point of greatest confusion and vulnerability. Did the romanticists really, as their words of warfare so clearly suggested, want their ideals to be brought into practice? Were they willing to stake their claim on the fact of an actual struggle? What element of reality was there to the romantic destructive illusion?

Carnegie probably knew the responses to his questions before he asked them. The romanticists were, finally, only after feelings of power and excitement; it was the rhetoric of war that mattered more than anything else—the rhetoric and the psychological affect. Carnegie recognized, too, the ambiguity in the romanticists' call to arms, their assertion of the "belligerent rights" of the dissatisfied, their insistence that "the axe must be laid at the roots of the trees of false life," but at the same time their equivocation when push came to shove, their final admission that all of this should be done only by "the strong arms of love."[29] What the romanticists wanted from their illusion of conquest was a return of honor, prestige, and deference, with as little of the reality of war as possible. And they got what they sought: the "splendid little war" against the "infidel" Spanish in the Caribbean, and the conquest and "liberation from barbarism" of the Philippines.[30]

The exaltation of war as the arena for romantic life and fulfillment had as its complement the valorization of knighthood and of courtly, chivalric virtue as the rule of romantic life. Knighthood was in vogue with a vengeance in the nineties. It provided the standard and model for the various cults of self-assertion, from paramilitary organizations to activist groups to youth athletic leagues. Above all, it provided a structured and successful image in which individuals could participate, a clear, forceful, and honorable definition of what it meant to be a self-made individual.[31]

The image of the knight represented not only forcefulness and honor but also, and perhaps more important, intensity and obedience. The knight, it was said, lived a life of unswerving allegience. He (or she)[32] was always once-born, with a faith that exemplified an unquestioning loyalty to higher authorities. All this faith and obedience, in turn, allowed for a life of constant tough action: the knight "practiced virtue in a rough and ready fashion which would not pass muster in modern society, though it might in Heaven."[33] Here again was the reactionary element of the image as it was drawn by the romanticists. The knightly hero, having sworn off the wayward patterns and convolutions of introspection, stood as a counterexample and antidote to the images of moribund individuals. The knight was neither a scholar nor a saint, both of those types being too riddled with dilemmas and vulnerabilities (usually caused, of course, by an excess of mental deliberation). Neither was he or she part of the palsied worlds of politics or business; these, after all, were dominated by questionable goals and a compromising spirit.[34] To be sure, the knightly self might enter into any one of these arenas, but not with any allegiance to them. Rather, they were like dragons' dens filled with a plunder that needed to be saved, and then left alone.

Understandings of the way and rule of knighthood did, of course, vary from one person to the next: one might emphasize the "hard" side of knighthood, with a stress on disciplined, martial bellicosity; another the "soft" side, highlighting the still uncompromising but now also benevolent idealism of knightly action. Whichever way the emphasis ran, however, a core of common definitions formed the nucleus of the knightly image. An individual of athletic virtue and prowess, always prepared for, indeed always seeking out, the high road of maximum exertion and adventure; a person who was clear-headed and with a soul at peace, facing straight ahead with a singleness of purpose: such were the characteristics held up as exemplary by romanticists of all persuasions during the nineties.

Despite its high regard for courtly codes of conduct, the depiction of the knightly self was not entirely medieval; rather, it was an odd mixture of medieval images laid atop a modern, liberal Protestant understanding of the human person. The meaning and end of the knightly life had to do not with the glorification of a greater God or good but with the attainment of a sense of personal authenticity and self-satisfaction. Combativeness and the questing spirit— the old time-honored virtues—were merged with contemporary concerns for self-realization and feelings of self-worth. "Because I am a child of God, made in his image," wrote Washington Gladden, stating clearly the modern logic of a self-centered universe, "I must highly value myself, I must hold my manhood in honor, I must seek, in every lawful way, to develop its powers, to enlarge its capacities of knowledge and of happiness; to make it what God meant it to be."[35] The knight of faith experienced no nights of faith in which human powers were placed in the balance and found wanting. To follow the knightly quest was to shore up and enlarge one's own ways and ends; it simply removed self-doubt rather than bringing it to a point of conviction and overturning.

There was a communal counterpart to the image of the knightly individual, a group image that mirrored that of the knight but was based on a heightened sense of racial and national identity. Usually, and almost always when the rhetoric was at its thickest, the image was painted in Anglo-Saxon hues: here was the race, or so it was claimed, that had steadily advanced and matured over the centuries and was now about to take its place as the dominant ruling group.[36] Sometimes, however, and increasingly as the 1890s came to a close, the image was drawn in terms of an American group, of a race forged from the superior Anglo-Saxon spirit but leavened by the more vital traits of other immigrant stock. In this version of the racialist romance, Americans had accrued and acquired all of the traits that were essential to a full and rich civilization. Liberty and spiritual religion; the ability to colonize and conquer; wisdom, power, and foresight in enterprise: whatever seemed valuable quickly became a national trait.[37]

Anglo-Saxonism and Americanism also gave a revitalized interpretation of history, an idea of the past, present, and future in which the feelings and acts of self-reaffirmation could be grounded. They provided a sense of continuity with a preindustrial and premodern past, what amounted to a kind of apostolic succession from (and hence back into) an uncompromising primitive racial age. As Walter Hines Page wrote in an editorial for his *Atlantic Monthly*:

> The race from which we are sprung is a race that for a thousand years has done the adventurous and outdoor tasks of the world. . . . Are we, by virtue of our surroundings, become a different people from our ancestors, or are we yet the same race of Anglo-Saxons, whose restless energy . . . has carried their speech into every part of the world, and planted their habits everywhere?[38]

Arguments about the past helped, in turn, to shore up images of the present state of racial and national identity; they offered a way out of the sense of the postwar decades that Americans, and Anglo-Saxon Americans in particular, had become overcivilized, too finely strung, and thus nerveless and neurasthenic. Racial and national images offered a countermodel. Like the call to arms of the warrior ideal, they functioned as goads to regeneration, reminders that the historic and higher vocation was still open, even to a generation "that has had no part in any adventure."[39] The cure for nervelessness was quite simple: Americans had only to return to what they once were.

The openness of the present to the past and the possibility of renewal by reversion to that past had as their end the creation of a grand myth about the future, an image of a new, resplendent, and above all inexorable Anglo-Saxondom. *Looking Backward*,[40] as Edward Bellamy called his account of the soon-to-be-present future world, projected one into a new utopia. A careful analysis of the inheritance of the past disclosed the images and shadows of that world just breaking across the horizon. And was it not true, asked Josiah Strong in *Our Country*, that "by the close of the next century, the Anglo-Saxons will outnumber all the other civilized races of the world? Does it not look as if God were not only preparing in our Anglo-Saxon civilization the die with which to stamp the peoples of the earth, but as if he were also massing behind that die the might with which to press it?"[41]

By the close of the nineteenth century, the romantic interpretation of the forces of inheritance and of past events had produced a new version of the American errand. It had to do not just with criticism and reform but with real deeds and action, enlargement, and mastery. Americans were being called away from their life of enslavement to routine occupations and fascination with morbid fictions; they were being called to an outgoing adventure of civilizing the world, of planting American habits everywhere. This errand came with its own guarantee: it was not an experiment or trial; it was not even a particularly risky venture; it had a clear promise of success and inevitable fulfillment. Albert Beveridge wrote: In "The March of the Flag,"

> It is a glorious history our God had bestowed upon His chosen people, a history heroic with faith in our mission and our future; a history of statesmen who flung the boundaries of the Republic out into unexplored lands and savage wilderness; a history of soldiers who carried the flag across blazing deserts and through the ranks of hostile mountains, even to the gates of sunset; a history divinely logical, in the process of whose tremendous reasoning we find ourselves today.[42]

The story of the American errand and mission, filled with fields of adventurous action and a cast of exemplary knightly individuals born of the Anglo-Saxon Adam, was told by many as the beginning of a new and final order of things—the opening of those wider democratic vistas that had been called for throughout the late nineteenth century. With its mythologization of the American race, it appeared to meet the demand, as Walt Whitman had stated in 1871, for an American saga with "a knightlier and more sacred cause" at its heart. And with its avowal of enormous national and racial destinies, it provided that "larger and grander work" that was said to be needed; it offered a story that was "more than the counterpart" of the destinies and stories of the grand old European races and nations.[43]

Just barely beneath the surface, however, the seemingly democratic vistas gave way to feudal, hierarchical ones: nobility, imperialism, the sovereign sway and authority of heaven-directed purposes—these were the determining words about the kind of errand that was to be run. Whitman and others had called for a story of the "average, the bodily, the concrete, the democratic, the popular"; they demanded a tale of the individual and of society on the open road. Romanticists replied with a story that dealt with the very high average, bedecked with armor, mythical and aristocratic; theirs was a tale of a knight set out on the conquest of some human grail. Romanticists used the language of democracy not to offset an outworn chivalric order but to reestablish it. They did not move beyond the feudal world but rather attempted to bring it back to life once again.

Underlying the themes of war, knighthood, and the flowering of the Anglo-Saxon stock was a religious theme, the story of ultimate fulfillment in a kingdom of God that both recapitulated the other, secular themes and brought them to their full and final end. The composition of the religious historical romance was, once again, a mixture of popular modern definitions and medieval, antimodern models. On the side of the modern, evolution, progress, efficiency, and what Lester Frank Ward called "sociocracy"[44] explained the drama that was unfolding. Exaggerated arguments about the extent and radicality of present and prospective changes gave movement to the story of religious advance. What was advancing, however, was a high medieval religious order, a kingdom of God the descriptions of which were steeped in monarchic titles and theocratic images, and which demanded absolute obedience to "the Lord Jesus

Christ as the supreme authority."[45] Forward evolution thus meant a reversion to an older order, progress a return to a purer, more primitive age of faith.

Another element of the religious romance needs to be mentioned, namely, its emphasis on spirituality as the one true form of religiosity. What was usually intended by this term was an understanding that religious truth resided in an inner, ideal realm. Talk about social change and movement was not for its own sake but rather for the sake of pointing up those images and shadows of the invisible in the visible realm. "Man is by divine purpose, by birth, and his true inheritance, free," said Horatio Dresser. "He must come forth and claim his freedom," he continued, but then added, lest the kind of freedom he was advocating be misunderstood, "the true freedom of his inner or spiritual nature."[46]

The effect of this tendency toward spiritualization on the religious story was to drive it heavenward. It turned the changes elaborated in the religious romance into the highest possible fictions of the real, tales told about the absorption of the timebound into the timeless and unalterable. Symptomatic of this upward direction in the religious story was the manner in which Jesus, now the hero and exemplar of the crusade for the pure and true, typically was depicted: he was at once the historical Jesus, the "great initiator of the Christian revolution," but also, and more important, the ethereal, world-transcending figure whose life and actions were finally secondary accretions to the "transparent clearness and peace of his soul."[47] To imitate Jesus, to follow in his steps, was to seek a path that led to a world once removed from the present, muddled religious situation. It was to move away from the human Jesus and toward a cosmic Christ.

The religious drama that emerged from this blending of modern, antimodern, and spiritualist elements had as its first and central story line the inevitable and almost ineluctable advance of Christian causes and forms of practice. As with the more general theme of war, here too religion was wrapped in a context of conquest: the tale spoke of a church both militant and triumphant, on the march, always undaunted in its strength and ever-accumulating power. Concomitantly, the Christian realm was depicted as a vast and spreading kingdom, governed by its sovereign Lord and King. There was no ambiguity in the spreading ecclesiastical scene; all appeared as a vital, spirit-indwelling city of a God without malice. Everything conspires, said Daniel Dorchester,

> to show that more than ever before God has a living church within the churches, towering amid them all in its mightiness,— the strength, the support, the central life of all; and that an increasing number of true believers are "walking with Him in white," a grand constellation of light and purity,—a bright Milky Way from earth to heaven.[48]

How this advance and triumph were to be made manifest was through the work of missions, the goal of which was not simply the winning of souls and new converts but nothing less than the complete restoration of "the kingdom of Heaven here and now."[49] Under the unity of the spirit, as some saw it, liberals, conservatives, and progressives found themselves allied in a grand foreign mission movement; they aimed for a world evangelized, Christianized, and civilized.[50] Similar projects were raised in terms of home missionary activity, where the goal was the reshaping of America into a theocratic, Christian nation. "The social problem," stated George Herron, "is the call of the state to become Christian. The state can save itself only by believing in the Lord Jesus Christ."[51]

This sense of mission, advance, and renovation was backed by an assertion about the present religious situation that proved the accuracy of missionary aspirations. Most of the globe, it was frequently noted, was already under at least the indirect influence of Christian forces; the expansion of the Western world eastward and southward inevitably would install a Christian order worldwide.[52] Significantly, the forces of Christianization and civilization were also those with the greatest secular power. As Sydney Gulick of the Missionary Board of Commissioners for Foreign Missions said in 1897: "Christianity is the religion of the dominant nations of the earth. Nor is it rash to prophesy that in due time it will be the only religion of the world."[53]

This rendering of the signs of the times, coupled with grand projections about the imminent future world, issued in inflated estimations about the kind of work to which the individual should be committed. Mission activity of all sorts was couched in the language of extraordinary heroics and magnificent deeds: believers were given a vision of themselves as "soldiers of the Kingdom of

God," fighters in the largest army that had ever been amassed.[54] The vision was one of a great medieval Crusade, with missionaries both at home and abroad bringing benighted lands and peoples into the daylight of the new world order. Indeed, for many it signified not just a return to the battle scene of the Middle Ages but its ultimate end, the Crusade to end all Crusades.

Depictions of the self as a militantly religious figure, and of the activity of missions as a crusading adventure, dovetailed with the general romantic story of war, conquest, and the knightly life. To fight for the Christianization and civilization of the world was no longer just to fight with the weapons of faith. Although these remained part of the "equipment of the soldiers of the Kingdom of God,"[55] there was now the added array of conventional and secular weapons of war. The whole notion of a social gospel and of Christian social action carried within its logic an understanding that the war of faith was a real war; like the Crusades of old, it would be fought out not from a position of separation from secular forces and powers but in, with, and through them.[56]

The obverse was that the romantic assessment of war and the knightly, master-race virtues were given a reduplication and a justification in a transcendent realm: secular logic—the dominance of Anglo-Saxondom, the valorization of aggressive martial values—now could be matched and merged with a divine logic. Set beside assertions that America was the most advanced civilization of the day, religious proclamations clinched the romantic argument for the greatness of its prospective way of life. In a word, they allowed for the identification of American ways with the ways of God.

This merging of secular and sacred themes emerged most clearly in the proposed end of the movement and advance, the establishment of what amounted to a new American City of God. "Democracy, whether industrial or political, is theocracy," stated George Herron,[57] and in that statement appeared the central element of the new world order. The drama of religious advance would reach its culmination when all governing forces, both secular and sacred, consented to the power and the sovereign rule of God. Democracy would convert to theocratic rule, or rather would become so democratic that it once again would become monarchical. Romantic fulfillment focused on the notions of kingship and empire: "As the idea of the kingdom is the key to the teachings and work of Christ," wrote Walter Rauschenbusch, "so its abandonment or misconstruction is the key to the false or one-sided conceptions of Christianity."[58]

What was given in this depiction of the triumphant theocratic realm, and more generally in the whole of the historical romance, was an image of magnitude and unity, in terms of both the projected ends to be gained and the adventures to be found along the way. The expansion of Christendom, like the expansion of American civilization and Anglo-Saxondom, was more than just a march of ever-greater numbers of followers. That provided intrigue; what gave the story its breadth and grandeur, however, was the vastness of the canopy under which all facets of life and all manner of peoples would shelter. "The revolution comes not to destroy, but to organize society with a divine and deathless life,"[59] stated George Herron, striking the dominant note in the mystical romantic chords. Unity and magnitude were simply unqualified goods; few asked what kind of fulfillment there would be for people under this world-embracing, heavenly dome.[60]

All of this emphasis on breadth and oneness may seem at odds with the stress on change and transformation. The historical romance did seek to depict a world set free and in process, something placed over against all that was settled. Romanticists perceived correctly that the daily rounds of life could, if they had not already done so, become a husk preventing any fresh shoots from appearing. But the imagined end subverted the emphasis on the freedom of change: the goal was not diversity and continual creation but uniformity; the process reached its culmination in a static and permanent order that would never again be altered. Having a need to serve the desire for security as well as for freedom, romanticists chose the freedom of security, rejecting outright the security of freedom.

This choice of security, in turn, emptied the historical romance of any opportunity it might have presented for critique. As the concern, above all else, was for a return to a stable order, so all differences of opinion were better left unresolved. "We do not ask what men believe," said Lyman Abbott, and as it has been pointed out, he could just as easily have substituted "care" for "ask."[61] Sentiments such as this left the romantic vision with no critical insight, no means of seeing what was and was not being proposed, no means of denying the symbols of ultimacy that were being affirmed. In the end, the historical romance could and did accommodate almost any set of values that might be put forth.

High-flying and auspicious, a world of adventuresome action where nothing could puncture the feeling of elation: such was the impression left by the historical romance. It all seemed a bit too high-flown, however, lacking an appreciation for the tenacity of facts and, more than that, incapable of understanding the inevitable misgivings and disinclincations that accompany action in the world, the fanaticisms and the irrationalities that govern the mind in and through its high ideals. When all was said and done, the new romanticism provided nothing more than a way of escape without any real need for commitment, a struggle that required nothing more than that one forget oneself under the enticement of an idea. The historical romance was simply a movement that, despite its claims about the need for sacrifice, had little risk and called for nothing to be given up.

America should have had to undergo its fate in the wake of the cultural collapse of the 1860s, 70s and 80s. It did not do so, but rather found a way around its task. The cost of this sidestepping was that, despite the boldness of the romanticists' claims—their promise of the rejuvenated self, the grandeur of their soon-to-be-realized new world order, and the intrigue of conquests and adventures—the romantic theme remained one of morbidness. To be sure, it was not the same theme that had been played in the 1860s, 70s, and 80s: aggression had taken the place of disintegration and nervelessness; visions of eternal, unalterable fulfillment had covered the gaps. But beneath the appeal to eternity, all remained the same: there was no confrontation with the facts. If romanticists saw, they resolutely refused to count the price that had to be paid for an attempt at real change. And thus they continued to be caught in the web they had sought to dispel. At its heart their story remained empty and unfulfilling. What they offered, finally, was only the continuing tale of a depressed and desolate self. All that had changed was that the self was now the aggressor out for vengeance.

4

The Self Resubmitted

All that is in the world is lust of the flesh, lust of the eyes or pride of life. Libido sentiendi, libido sciendi, libido dominandi. Wretched is the cursed land consumed rather than watered by these three rivers of fire! Happy are those who are beside those rivers, not standing but sitting, in a low and safe position. They will not rise thence before the light, but, after resting in peace, stretch out their hands to him who shall raise them to stand upright and steady in the porches of Jerusalem the blessed, where pride shall no more be able to fight against them and lay them low; and yet they weep, not at the sight of all the perishable things swept away by these torrents, but at the memory of their beloved home, the heavenly Jerusalem, which they constantly remember through the long years of their exile.   Blaise Pascal, *Pensées*

Once and only once William James played the part of a public orator. It was on May 31, 1897, at the Boston Music Hall, on the occasion of the unveiling of a war memorial to Colonel Robert Gould Shaw.[1] The oration was, by James's own admission, not very distinguished: "The task is a mechanical one," he complained in a letter to Benjamin Paul Blood, "and the result somewhat of a school-boy composition."[2] There was also something slightly incongruous about James's presence in the midst of this public celebration of war. Here was James the neurasthenic (the persistence of this malady was evidenced by a case of laryngitis contracted a few days before the ceremony) being paraded in martial splendor through the streets of Boston, "toted around," as he put it, "for two hours in a barouche at the end of a procession."[3] And here was

James standing before the assembled gathering of soldiers and citizens, speaking about a colonel in a war from which James had been excused, and about which the only firsthand experience he had was a sight of the smoke from a burning Richmond glimpsed as he passed along the coast on a boat bound for South America and an academic expedition. James managed to make something of his turn before the public eye, although as he wrote to his brother Henry, the whole affair was "entirely outside of my own line of business."[4]

Fortunately for James, there was something equally incongruous about Colonel Shaw and the fact that a statue had been cast in his image. "Poor little Robert Shaw," William James wrote to Henry, "erected into a symbol of deeper things than he ever realized himself,—the tender grace of a day that is dead, etc."[5] Shaw's atypical and, by military standards, far less than successful career gave James something to talk about—something, moreover, that with the rise of the new romanticism had become a matter of some importance to him. James took as his theme for the oration what amounted to the antiheroics of Shaw and his Fifty-fourth Regiment. He aimed his praise at the fact that the statue now being unveiled was "the first soldier's monument to be raised to a particular set of comparatively undistinguished men."[6]

"How, indeed, comes it," James asked his audience, "that out of all the great engagements of the war, engagements in many of which the troops of Massachusetts had borne the most distinguished part, only a young colonel, this regiment of black men and its maiden battle,—a battle, moreover, which was lost,—should be picked out for such unusual commemoration?" Certainly there could be no pretending that Shaw had come close to resembling the popular ideal of the knight of war; he had led a group of "outcasts," and his sole military accomplishment was that he had marched his soldiers in vain "up the parapet of Fort Wagner, where he and nearly half of them were left upon the ground." Only with effort and a measure of irony could one pull from Shaw's life and death, and the story of his command, some tale of martial strength. As James explained it, if the statue before his listeners was a monument, it was to something other than war and the usual soldier's story; if it stood as a tribute, it was to a marginal fact, something to be recalled only "after the great generals have had their monuments, and long after the abstract soldier's monuments have been reared on every village green."[7]

James returned to his central and opening point: it was, or at least it should be, the "very lack of external complication in the history of these soldiers" that made them worthy of representation and commemoration. Similarly, it was not that Shaw was a paragon of martial prowess and tactical skill which provided the occasion for remembering his life and actions. There was, to be sure, a virtue celebrated by Saint Gaudens's statue, but it was only coincidental with the fact of war. Common civic courage was the name James gave that virtue: faithfulness to a cause (here the cause of the fight against racism and slavery), the willingness to suffer ridicule, abuse, and failure in the performance of one's tasks. And with specific regard to Colonel Shaw, what was worthy of being recalled was that he had relinquished his chance at real military success and acclaim, that having "till then been walking socially on the sunny side of life," he had decided "to risk worldly fortunes all alone in resisting an enthroned abuse."[8]

It thus would be better, James continued, to commemorate Shaw and his Fifty-fourth not as conquering heroes but as saints of a religious faith, lonely followers of what James called "our American religion," namely, that "a man requires no master to take care of him, and that common people can work out their own salvation well enough together if left free to try." Indeed, to view the Shaw monument as a war memorial would be to dismiss the kind of battle that Shaw and his command had really fought. "War," James said, "has been much praised and celebrated among us of late as a school of manly virtue; but it is easy to exaggerate upon this point. . . . What we really need the poet's and orator's help to keep alive in us is that more lonely courage which he showed when he dropped his warm commission in the glorious Second."[9]

There was one other point to James's address: having reversed the image of Shaw both from a warrior to a saint and from a hero to a mundane figure, he now completed the turn by recalling what it was that any war memorial should properly be about. After all the soldierly accolades had been played out, what stood before them, said James, was not an expression of the grandeur of war nor a reminder of any intrinsic worth of conflict in human affairs.

Rather, here was a memorial to the tragedy of war, to the squandering of life that was the inevitable outcome of all calls to arms. What the monument should have brought to memory was not some scene of victorious battlers but the "yellow bleached photographs" of those who had fought and died. And what needed to be recalled was the "interminable concreteness" of an event that had become little more than "an abstract name, a picture, a tale that is told."[10] Only then would the war memorial have made its proper point, namely, that there was no point to war, and that beneath the glory of wartime endeavor there was always a stark side that had as its outcome only waste.

There is only so much that can be said about James's address on Robert Shaw. It was not a particularly distinguished oration; although it had its points, they were not the sort that were intended to bear a great deal of reflective weight. At the risk of overburdening, however, one more comment needs to be made, about the relationship between the depiction of Shaw and James's other work and writings. What James offered in his portrait of Shaw was a counter to the redescribed self that had been presented in the *Principles* and that had exploded in the late nineteenth century. Whereas before James's emphasis had been on the self of assertion, filled with the chance at adventure and heroic action, now the reverse was stressed: loneliness, submission and suffering for the sake of a cause, risk, failure, and antiheroics. And where formerly James had placed his image in a theater of possibility, on a stage set high and brightly lit, here the surroundings were dark hued, a stage for tragedy rather than romance. James portrayed Shaw as an example of fulfillment not through assertion but through relinquishment, an example of gaining life by handing over one's fortunes.

This shift in perspective was not accidental but indicative, characteristic of James's turn of thought throughout the 1890s. One need only review the topics of his work during this period—degeneration and genius, exceptional mental states, the risks of faith, the varieties of religious experience—to notice the trend.[11] The same shift can be seen in terms of James's social concerns and commitments: his antiwar and anti-imperial sentiments; his defense of religious therapists against the attacks of the medical establishment; his stance against a resurgent racism and white supremacy.[12]

The Shaw address is representative of the direction of James's thought after the *Principles*, and above all of his effort to give his definition of the self some "other roots besides wanton exuberance of imagination and perversity of heart."[13] We may leave the address at that and turn to the deeper investigations to which Shaw stood as a surface reflection.

Where James searched to find those other roots was in all that about the self which, in the *Principles*, he had been trying to overcome: its depression, its ambivalence and sense of tragedy, the insanity at the heart of its collapse. James returned to and developed a deeper regard for what he called the wider self, the marginal and ultramarginal facts of personal life, trance states, hallucinations, experiences of and convictions about subliminal selves. His work with the Society for Psychical Research had convinced him of the importance of all of these so-called fringe states in personal life; as he wrote in an 1892 article on the society, their findings "have broken down for my own mind the limits of the admitted order of things. Science, so far as science denies such exceptional occurrences, lies prostrate in the dust for me; and the most urgent intellectual need which I feel at present is that science be built up again in a form in which such things may have a positive place."[14]

Regard for the wider self had as its initial outgrowth for James's definition of the self a broadening of the notion of consciousness. The self was fully a confluence of innumerable streams now, James stated in his 1896 Lowell lectures, a "polyzoism or polypsychism."[15] Some of these streams resided above the threshold of ordinary waking awareness; they formed, as had been the case in the *Principles*, the dominant fields of consciousness and provided the base for the common habits and patterns of active assertion. Yet other streams, and for James now by far the most important ones, flowed along the margin of awareness, erupting only occasionally. It was usual (and by this James meant scientifically accepted) to discount these streams as meaningful; they were customarily consigned to the nether realms of pathological states and delusions. But, warned James, we neglected them at our peril, for it was the marginal in life that was determinative. "So get a clear idea of this one fundamental fact! The sound mind is a system of ideas in gear, integrated with every other idea, and having a field, a focus, and a margin; the margin, however, controls."[16]

James understood his emphasis away from the ordinary and dominant and toward the exceptional and marginal aspects of consciousness as a shift not only to more fundamental but also to more profound levels of existence. Recognition of and experience on the inner fringe of life brought the self face to face with wide and, in a sense, independent frameworks of meaning; it gave the possibility of a "more" to existence, of something broader than the assertions constructed by ordinary consciousness.[17] To live in recognition of the wider self was to live in confrontation with facts of experience that were in many ways beyond the self's control: it entailed a risk and a strenuousness born of insecurity; it put the self into a position of having to accept or reject rather than assert or recast.

Appreciation for the marginal facts of experience led in turn to an increased reappreciation of an almost lunatic vision of life, far away from the easy optimism of the hero, whose only task was to carve out his or her own world, and more in line with the vision of the melancholic and pessimist, in which there was a due recognition of both the wildness of freedom and the radicality of human insecurity. The melancholic, the neurasthenic, and the suicidal individuals of the 1860s now stood in James's redefinition as those who saw the sham in self-assertion, the tragic fragility of human constructions, the illusion of thinking that one could just set one's own course. In turn, these were the people who saw fit to forsake the rewards of the ordinary life ideals for the sake of wider meanings: "We speak of melancholy and morbid tendencies, but he would be a bold man who should say that melancholy was not an essential part of every character. Saint Paul, Lombroso, Kant, each is in some way an example of how melancholy in a life gives a truer sense of values. A life healthy on the whole must have some morbid elements."[18]

James's point in all of this was not to exalt the states of morbidity and dread; these remained problems that had to be passed through and, in a way, overcome. To the extent that he did regard them as exemplary, however, it was because they indicated an awareness of the contingency of life and of the need to hold to that awareness. The pessimist recognized, as did no other, just "how desperately difficult it is to construe the scientific order of nature either theologically or poetically."[19]

To fall prey to melancholy was thus to be able to see the world as, for James, it really was, fraught with equivocal facts, with meanings in need of something more. That was not just sickness but the first sign of health, the initial step beyond a state of tedium and also beyond the illusion of seeing oneself as essentially the creator of one's heroic realm. To be sure, the optimist would view all this as a matter of blindness, as a refusal to see that one can do away with the problems of not having any grounding in life, indeed, can therefore create at will. But, James argued, such was not the case. It was the melancholic who, in all of his or her apparent blindness, saw clearly; it was the optimist, particularly the late nineteenth-century optimist, who had forgotten that contingency also had to do with the self.[20]

Where, finally, all of this emphasis and stress on the "lonely depths" emptied out was in a new definition of the religious nature of the self, a reassessment both of the needs that bound the self and of the deliverance from their binding. Melancholy and pessimism were, at bottom, essentially religious diseases, cravings of the heart for a meaning wider than the self could by itself project or provide. Whereas in the *Principles* religious disease had been construed merely as a weakness of the will, a failure and a lack that could and should be overcome by habitual action and a stronger self-reliance, now, in the mid-nineties, James gave it a positive construction. Religious disease, the grubbing in the roots of things, became an almost necessary preliminary to any "communion with the soul of things"; James gave it the same status that revivalists gave the moods of religious preparation and conviction. What the pessimist knew, James argued, the truth that the melancholic had attained from his or her pain and fear, was that existence called not for a show of control but for an acquiescence to the free—and hence, for the human who would be autonomous, tragic—flow in which individual life was embedded.

Corresponding to James's deepening of the notion of the religious need of the human self was a re-evaluation of the cure for that need, of the meaning and logic of religious remedies and responses. Again, in the *Principles* religious life had been almost wholly a matter of the self's creative activity, a kind of self-binding in which a religious reality was posited and then sustained by the self. Religious belief, in turn, was for all practical purposes simply a labeling and defense of certain experiences as ultimate. By the mid-nineties, however, all of this had changed, or had at least been altered by the addition of a possible binding power alongside the self. Religious belief was now an act of assertion but sometimes also of submission. It involved deliverance as well as the construction of a religious reality. James's famous "will to believe" had to do both with willfulness and willingness, assertion and resignation.[21] It was the outgrowth of a communication, a dialogue with another and wider (though not deeper) reality rather than just a monologue with oneself. Significantly, this religious reality was not, for James, something independent of the self; it remained a wider self, "a wider spiritual life with which our superficial consciousness is continuous." But the continuity now had the character of a confrontation, a "commerce" as James put it, a meeting more than a mere exhibition of self-assertion and creativity.[22]

As the nature of religious belief shifted, so too did the understanding of religious experience, and in the same direction. In James's new definition religious experience encompassed both passive and active experiences; James talked not only of particular, marginal experiences but also of a "God of those particular experiences." "If you ask what these experiences are," he said, "they are conversations with the unseen, voices and visions, responses to prayer. . . . The power comes and goes and is lost, and can be found only in a certain direction."[23] Whereas in the *Principles* the religious quality of experience was wholly a matter of the self's naming an experience as binding, now the impetus for naming, and in a sense the actual denomination, came from without. Religious experience was fast becoming an experience of the self being bound.

This shift in perspective and understanding may seem to be leading back into the very "wanton exuberance" that James had initially intended to overcome. Conversations with the unseen, commerce with a wider self, hallucinations: all of these appear to be but a fine line away from the "perverted ideal emotions" that James found so wrongheaded in his hero-bound age.[24] James, needless to say, argued that such was not the inevitable end of his new formulations. While his was still a "humanizing mission," it was one that could not slip over into self-aggrandizement. The grounding in the tragic dimension of human life was too strong for that. And although he continued to sympathize with the romanticists in their struggle to find an alternative to the emptinesses of positivism and materialism (indeed, he called his new point of view a "personal and romantic view of life"),[25] he had taken ultimacy out of the hands of the self.

To begin with, James felt that he had reined in his definition, given it limits enough to work against any "easy excursions into the unseen that other people make at the bare call of sentiment."[26] From the side of the ordinary conscious self, the whole notion of an experience of divinity was predicated on the understanding of human impossibility, of the yawning gap, unbridgeable by the self alone, between the human and the tentatively labeled divine. Thus, while James held out "an environment so romantic as to baffle all one's habitual sense of teleology and moral meaning," he simultaneously stressed that this environment was not a haven and could never be a home. "The world is evidently more complex than we are accustomed to think it," he wrote. It was increasingly difficult to dismiss even some of the more "fantastic prolongations of mental life into the unknown." But then he added, in further explanation, that part of the complexity was due to the fact that these experiences forced one to see the divine, the "absolute world-ground," as "being further off than it is the wont either of the usual empiricisms or of the usual idealisms to think it."[27]

Claims to experiences of divinity thus always involved maybe's and risks: "Like all other human experiences, they too certainly share in the general liability to illusion and mistake." The most that could be said of them was that they were "the originals of the God idea"; there was a point of identification but no point of identity.[28] This, along with the fact that all these experiences were only personal and had to be set in the context of the varieties of religious experience, led to an attitude of tolerance and respect for the plurality of other claims to divinity. It also protected against the rise of a crusading, self-righteous campaign.

Side by side with the insistence on tolerance and a respect for the plurality of experience went a stress on the contingent nature of experience. Conversations with the unseen were always experiences of an unknown, real but not necessarily true; they could thus be evaluated only in terms of their results and effects. The "healthiness"[29] of a life lived in reference to the subliminal and unseen, James argued, striking at the roots of what would later become his conception of pragmatism, had to be judged by the experience's practical value for life—practical in the sense of liveliness, that is, in terms of how it played itself out. As James stated in his Lowell lectures:

> There is no purely objective standard of sound health. We are all instruments for social use, and if sensibilities, obsessions and other psychopathic peculiarities can so combine with the rest of our constitution as to make us the more useful to our kind, why, then, we should not call them in that context points of unhealthiness, but rather the reverse.[30]

All of these formulations, new directions, and proposals ran rather roughly in James's thought throughout the nineties. The facts of exceptional and marginal experience sat collected but not yet sorted and understood; the pluralistic and pragmatic checks and balances had been given an initial statement but not a thorough development and application. It was as if all the images and elements of James's marginal and extramarginal self were present but had not yet been brought into a unified portrait. And the methods of depiction, although defined as being in the service of practical life and activity, had been given little by way of specific explication.

Where, finally, all of these formulations and new images began to come together was in James's Gifford lectures on religious experience, which would be delivered as *The Varieties of Religious Experience*.[31] Here James offered a fully developed definition of the religious individual, a model of the "saint" that showed clearly James's effort to provide a middle ground between the extremes of the romantic constructions of self-assertion and the deadening, lifeless images of the positivists.[32] Also, in these lectures James gave a clear description and working model of his method of investigation, its principles, aims, and goals. The science of religions, which he had called for throughout the 1890s as a critical lever against the religious romance, now had a definite expression as a kind of naturalistic theory of religion, an account and evaluation of the religious life of the self.[33]

It is usual in treatments of James's Gifford lectures to view them as more or less unrelated to his psychology, a brief excursion into the world of religious phenomena that should be understood as a version of the Jamesian "moral holiday." James allowed his tender-minded side a moment of play, or so the argument customarily runs. This recess came with the *Varieties*, which had neither antecedent nor postcedent.[34] As the foregoing discussion has begun to show, and as I will continue to explain, the move from the *Principles* to the Gifford lectures was properly a transition rather than a disruption; it has been the usual treatment of James, and not his *Varieties*, that is out of sync with James's emphases and work. *The Varieties of Religious Experience* is best understood as a kind of third volume to James's psychology, a continuing exploration of the marginal streams of consciousness and of their impact on the definition and depiction of the self of ordinary consciousness.

This continuity appeared at the outset of the lectures, both in James's description of the approach to religion that would be taken and, more important, in his circumscription of the topic of religious experience. James prefaced his lectures with the statement that he approached his topic as a psychologist. This meant that, as in the *Principles*, the method of investigation would be descriptive, and would be concerned with "religious feelings and religious impulses" rather than religious institutions.[35] Also, he would take as his working hypothesis an understanding that these feelings and impulses were of a "lowly origin": his perspective would be of the common sense sort found in the natural sciences, namely, that all religious phenomena proceeded from "organic conditions." This was not, James reminded his audience, to take a stance with what he called the "medical materialists," those who, in addition to insisting on organic conditions, also slipped in a negative judgment on the value of religious notions. As in the *Principles*, now too there would be no reduction to the organic, only a recognition that, descriptively, common sense demanded a self construed with "psycho-physical connections."[36]

The explanation of the approach to be taken led, in turn, to an introductory word about who it was that the lectures would deal with, and what was meant by religious life and religious experience. In choosing his subject matter, James would, as usual, draw upon testimony of a common, everyday variety: "The *documents humains* which we shall find most instructive need not then be sought for in the haunts of special erudition—they lie along the beaten highway." If the testimony was common, however, the persons giving the testimony were uncommon, odd, even extreme. Here James introduced his antiheroes of the 1860s, the morbid, despondent, *détraqué* individuals who had touched the lonely depths. It was characteristic of such people, James said, that they had been subject to abnormal psychical "visitations": "They have known no measure, been liable to obsessions and fixed ideas; and frequently have fallen into trances, heard voices, seen visions, and presented all sorts of peculiarities which are ordinarily classed as pathological."[37]

James gave two reasons for his choice of such persons as his subjects in the lectures. First, they tended to have had religious experiences at firsthand (unlike the ordinary believer, who usually gained his or her religion secondhand, by imitation): "We must search for the original experiences which were the pattern-setters. . . . These experiences we can only find in individuals for whom religion exists not as a dull habit, but as an acute fever rather." Second, and more to the point, only these subjects, in all their melancholy and eccentricity, exhibited what for James was the "essential moment in every complete religious evolution," namely, the "passionate resignation" and "spurning" of the ordinary world of awareness.[38]

This description moved James toward the preliminary explanation of what he meant by religious life and religious experience, what it was that constituted the "differentia" of religion, "the character of religious experience that is perfectly distinct." The addition of religion to life, James stated, was an attitude of freedom born out of acquiescence, a recognition of the helplessness of the self, its contingent and tragic situation, but along with that a perception of a "new sphere of power" beyond the self:

> There is a state of mind, known to religious men, but to no others, in which the will to assert ourselves and hold our own has been displaced by a willingness to close our mouths and be as nothing in the floods and waterspouts of God. In this state of mind, what we most dreaded has become the habitation of our safety, and the hour of our moral death has turned into our spiritual birthday.[39]

As James concluded the circumscription of his topic, he reminded his listeners once again that it was not his intent to array his exceptional personalities either for the sake of spectacle or for their own, eccentric sake. Religious persons, with all of their ventures into the unseen, were more than just an extreme case and an oddity; in their extremity they displayed for all to see the underside of every human life and experience. What the person of religious conviction provided, precisely because it came in so extraordinary a form, was a glimpse of currents and experiences that ran through all individuals. The religious genius seemed peculiar, indeed something of a freak; but the source of his or her exceptionality lay in the degree rather than the fact of religious commitment and concern.

To study the varieties of religious experience was thus to study, in its clearest and most manifest cases, the existential need of, and perhaps also a cure for, the normal self: it was to add another and necessary chapter to the psychology of the self. To emphasize the religiously infirm individual, bogged down in desperation, was to offer a fuller portrait of the ordinary person than was usually given in scientific studies. All of us, James argued, are in fact and at bottom open to incursions from a wider realm; we do not get along without some sort of religious rooting, for our everyday life is stamped with impossibility, an inability to gain a place of permanency and rest. And it is stamped so strongly that none of us can live all of the time under the illusion of being in control. "The sanest and best of us are of one clay with lunatics and prison-inmates . . . all our morality appears but as a plaster hiding a sore it can never cure, and all our well-doing as the hollowest substitute for that well-being that our lives ought to be grounded in, but, alas! are not."[40]

These arguments could only prepare the themes for James's later lectures; as he had done in his psychology, so here too he used his introductory words to set the stage for what was now his theater of religious possibility. Further elucidation would require a softening of the religious themes: the extravagances would have to be toned down so that they might exhibit their value for life overall. More to the point, the whole theater of religious life as James had arranged it would have to confront certain counterclaims and competing scenarios. The reality of the unseen—what, exactly, James meant by this universe upon which human personality depended—would have to be explained. Above all (and here James continued the battle that he had begun in the nineties), sense would have to be made of the religiously "healthy-minded," those for whom religious experience was all in the affirmative, for whom religion was a will to believe in the simple sense of self-assertion. Was religion the struggle to surrender that James claimed it to be, an outgrowth of an essentially unresolvable situation of contingency? Or was it only a matter of the self's creative power, an easygoing attitude that backed our assertions?

What James meant by the reality behind religious belief was, at its most general, simply a widened notion of the perception or sentiment of reality that had been presented in the *Principles*. It was "one of the cardinal facts in our human constitution" that our minds are determined by abstractions. These magnetize and polarize our lives. "We turn towards them and from them, we seek them, hold them, hate them, bless them, just as if they were so many concrete things." Here was the fundamental fact of psychology from which the notion of religious realities could be understood. "It is as if there were in the human consciousness a sense of reality, a feeling of objective presence, a perception of what we may call 'something there,'" more deep and more general than any of the special and particular 'senses' by which the current psychology supposes existent realities to be originally revealed."[41]

The realities upon which religious beliefs were founded, of course, were far more definite than this dim sentiment of a general, diffused reality that this larger sense yielded; religion, James explained, had to do with living gods and not just abstract ideals. Religious beliefs sprang from experiences best classified as "hallucinations," beyond rationality, presenting beings of an "ontological imagination." Without commenting on the truth of such experiences, James concluded: "We may now lay it down as certain that in the distinctively religious sphere of experience, many persons . . . possess the objects of their belief, not in the form of conceptions which their intellect accepts as true, but rather in the form of quasi-sensible realities directly apprehended."[42] From the descriptive, existential stance that James had adopted in the lectures, the unseen appeared as a psychological fact; it had to be accepted as real in its own, psychological sphere. There was a nonrational and subconscious stream in the self which, although its efficacy could be questioned, could not be denied on the grounds of factuality.

This conception of an unseen reality polarizing, magnetizing, and binding the self led James to an initial, prospective, and evaluative point, and in turn, back to his discussion of the fundamental religious types. If, as James had defined it, religion meant not only an object of belief constructed and appropriated by the self, but also a binding of the self by the religious object, then some conclusions could be drawn about the quality of religious experience and the reality of the unseen. Religious experiences that were the most complete were those that bounded most of the self's world, that encompassed sadness as well as joy, submission as well as exaltation—in a word, more of the complexities of human experience rather than fewer. James's final verdict on this point would wait until after his explanation of the two primary religious types. But at least here it stood as the introductory word to his description of those whose religious life cast out tragedy and contingency.

"The lustre of the present hour is always borrowed from the background of possibilities it goes with,"[43] James stated in one of his later lectures. I quote it here because it stood as the interpretive key for his assessments of the various religious types, and in this context of the healthy-minded believer. What James meant by the religiously healthy-minded were those who systematically denied the existence of contingency, relativism, and possible evil, whose "sky-blue optimism" was built on a conscious rejection of any experience of life as "curdling cold and gloom." In its established forms, which for James included liberalism, popular evolutionism, and the host of New Thought and Mind Cure movements, healthy-mindedness was a fiction grown to "a deliberate religious policy, or *parti pris*."[44] "Youth, Health, Vigor," a Mind Cure motto, meant for James nothing more than the active assertion of a world view that simply stepped over and around the fact of failure.

None of this, James said, was absurd; healthy-mindedness was an attitude "consonant with important currents in human nature." Everyone to at least some extent limited his or her view of the background of contingency; we all tend to "exult in the heroic opportunity and adventure." And experiences of unsullied identity with one's divine nature and good, all that from which the healthy-minded attitude was forged, were undeniable psychological facts: "These states of consciousness of 'union' form a perfectly definite class of experiences."[45] Above all, a life lived in a healthy-minded way provided results. To follow the practical imperatives of the optimist—for instance, "God is well and so are you"—was to revive a sense of personal efficacy, which, in its turn, had been shown to be justified by feats of individual achievement.

But maxims such as this, James continued, were also deceptive and dangerous, "pregnant with passports beyond the bounds of conventional morality." To begin with, the simple identification of God, the good, and the self was too easy, erected on a foundation of forgetting. The optimist's "contentment with the finite incases him like a lobster-shell and shields him from all morbid repining at his distance from the Infinite." And the healthy-minded gospel somehow lacked integrity; it was suspiciously defiant, all too often seeming to consist only of "bravado and an affected twist." To recognize this lack of integrity, one did not need to subscribe to an outlook bound by the morbid and melancholic. It was enough simply to adopt a perspective of measured realism.[46]

What, above all else, was so misleading about healthy-minded religiousness, however, was that it could not admit the possibility of failure, the negation so inevitably and inextricably bound up with life's successes and accomplishments. Experiences of failure, James argued, in which the "breath of the sepulchre" surrounded one's achievements, were not trifling moments but rather "pivotal human experiences"; almost always, they formed the "inmost consciousness" of the self, even of the happiest people: "Failure, then, failure! so the world stamps us at every turn. We strew it with our blunders, our misdeeds, our lost opportunities, with all the memorials of our inadequacy to our vocation. And with what a damning emphasis does it then blot us out."[47]

To be sure, James went on, failure may not be the final word, thought it is almost always the last: common sense holds that it is only natural to look out on the world and see the ultimates of everyday experience as facts of sadness. Stated in the extreme, which James saw as represented in the positivistic and agnostic streams of philosophy, human life was like living on the thin ice of a thawing lake, with the day drawing near when all would fall through and drown ignominiously. "The merrier the skating, the warmer and more sparkling the sun by day, and the ruddier the bonfires at night, the more poignant the sadness with which one must take in the meaning of the total situation."[48]

Thus, James concluded, healthy-mindedness was again not so much wrong as it was incomplete, a "fragile fiction," a "bell with a crack." And its incompleteness manifested itself precisely at the point where everyone had to stake his or her all, where the world judged one *in actu* and not just *in posse*. Life "seems infected with a contradiction." The failure of human constructions was one of the inescapable and, for James, essential facts of experience, one that could be ignored only at our peril. To anyone who admitted the facts of failure, healthy-mindedness was, finally, insufficient: "To ascribe religious value to mere happy-go-lucky contentment with one's brief chance at natural good is but the very consecration of forgetfulness and superficiality. Our troubles lie indeed too deep for *that* cure."[49]

James ended his analysis of healthy-mindedness by rejecting not only its depth of outlook but also its religious status. Its sins of omission left it not simply shortsighted but without the power of binding. In those despondent days and dark nights that everyone experienced, it was not enough just to think on the rare moments of being bathed in the springs of delight. As James turned to his analysis of the sick-souled religious type, he did so leaving healthy-mindedness characterized as a partial, penultimate type of religious life, one that gained its luster by avoidance, by slipping past the disagreeable facts. Complete religious life did not disdain the range of possible facts, good and evil. If it gained a perspective on the positive side of life, it did so not by forgetting and by ignoring but by granting the reality of the tenuousness of things.

Not much more needs to be said about James's sick-souled self, for by now the outlines of this religious type should already by clear.[50] A few points, however, do require some statement. First, with the lecture on the sick-soul James finally began his positive portrait of the new psychological and religious self. The previous lectures had, in the main, functioned to clear the ground of potential misunderstandings and reigning popular images of religious individuals; they provided the background for, and opened the contrasts to what would become, the saintly self. James's alternative to the "smooth and lying official conversational surface" was the self of desperation and anxiety. As he stated, rather offhandedly: "So we note here the neurotic constitution, of which I said so much in my first lectures, making its active entrance on our scene, and destined to play a part in much that follows."[51]

What James added to his earlier image of the religious self was a more exaggerated description both of the nature of religious need and of the kind of cure required to meet that need. The sick-souled self was not just mildly melancholic but pathologically so, an individual with an all-embracing sensitivity to the negative in life, an "extremity of pessimism."[52] Questions of purpose, meaning, and result, and, more important, the unavailability of any but contingent answers to these questions, were for James's model not minor problems but dread crises and obsessions. Using Tolstoy as his example of the sick-souled type, James said:

> At first it seemed as if such questions must be answerable . . . but as they ever became more urgent, he perceived that it was like those first discomforts of a sick man, to which he pays but little attention until they run into one continuous suffering, and then he realizes that what he took for a passing disorder means the most momentous thing in the world for him, means his death.[53]

Concomitant with the images of pain and fear, and of the wretchedness that the sick-souled self laid bare, there was in James's depiction an image of a self with a divided world and will. The truly religious individual, James explained, was one for whom the world appeared as a "double-storied mystery." Good, for such a person, was "not simply insufficient in amount and transient, there lurks a falsity in its very being." And within the self was a similar doubleness, a disposition of the will to set the self over against itself. "Wrong living, impotent aspirations; 'What I should, that do I not; but what I hate, that I do,' as Saint Paul says; self-loathing, self-despair, an unintelligible and intolerable burden to which one is mysteriously the heir."[54]

It should be noted that throughout this depiction James continued to remind his listeners that, extreme as the images he was drawing were, they depicted neither a deluded nor even a particularly unusual personality. There ought to be in all of us a recognition of the correctness of the sick-soul's convictions, for such lunatic visions were "all drawn from the materials of daily fact." If they seemed odd and stretched, it was not from any disability but rather from an exceptional ability to confront the contingency of life. And the sick-soul's understandings about the nature of things had a familiar kind of appropriateness; there was a common wisdom in all the tragic perceptions and beliefs. "There is no need of more examples," James concluded after having explained what was his own melancholic experience. "The cases we have looked at are enough. One of them gives us the vanity of mortal things; another the sense of sin; and the remaining one describes the fear of the universe,—and in one of these three ways it always is that man's original optimism and self-satisfaction get levelled with the dust."[55]

What all of this sickness of the soul resulted in for James was a depiction of the cure the self required. The radical melancholic, who saw tragedy and contingency at the root of things, could not be healed by an alteration of his or her everyday environment or by some shifting of the habits of the inner self. All of that was far too human. What was required was, in a sense, a supernatural remedy.[56] To such a person, after all, the natural order was disunified, disintegrated. With recourse only to this order, any cure would simply worsen the disease. When consciousness told the sick-soul that all was not well, James explained, urgings to believe in a better world could not mean much. Beliefs like that were at best fictions, more likely lies: "cold-blooded falsehoods," as James put it. "The will to believe cannot be stretched that far. We can make ourselves more faithful to a belief of which we have the rudiments, but we cannot create a belief out of whole cloth when our perception actively assures us of the opposite."[57]

Salvation of some sort was needed. The sick-souled self, because it was bound to such an all-embracing recognition, had to have a wider unifying boundary if it was to be secure. "The process," James said, "is of redemption, not of mere reversion to natural health, and the sufferer, when saved, is saved by what seems to him a second birth, a deeper kind of conscious being than he could enjoy before."[58] The sick-soul stood convicted of the deep contingency of life: there was no way to turn to that life again for help. What was required was a conversion, a turning to and with a larger framework of meaning.

This talk about redemption, however, had a very specific meaning; it was not simply some birth to a new world apart from the old but a conjoining of a "more," a wider life, with all that life was already. The necessary religious response, when it came, did not

bring the happiness of the once-born and healthy-minded; it provided no blinders against the tragic, but rather a recognition of
tragedy as included in its broader insight. Redemption was a stimulus, a faith, a reinfused willingness to live, and a new center of
action, all within a full recognition of the "perceptions that erewhile
made life seem unbearable." Those who had reached the point of
James's melancholy "had drunk too deeply of the cup of bitterness
ever to forget its taste, and their redemption is into a universe two-
stories deep."[59]

This depiction of redemption as a conjunction of an old and new
life had implications beyond just the retention of a contingent and
tragic point of view: it meant that the whole of the self as it had
been prior to redemption was preserved. Stated in terms of James's
image of the self, religious redemption, while certainly adding
another dimension to the image of the natural, everyday self, did
not re-create that image in the process of renovation; neither did it
override the principles of that self's formation. Conversion, that
turning point of religious life, was neither miraculous nor, strictly
speaking, transformative.[60] Whatever the case may have been with
regard to supernatural agency in the process, it was also a matter of
natural psychology; conversion took place in, with, and under the
natural conditions of the self. Shifts in patterns of association, the
building up of new habits of attention, changes of focus in the fields
of consciousness: these were the necessary first characterizations of
the conversion of the self. As James put it: "To say that a man is
'converted' means, in these terms, that religious ideas, previously
peripheral to his consciousness, now take a central place, and that
religious aims form the habitual center of his energy."[61]

Conversion thus construed as conditioned by natural psychological processes said nothing, of course, about the possible workings
from an extramental realm. The turning of the sick soul to a new
vital center could be described as a turning effected by a wider,
distinct self. Natural psychological descriptions, after all, could not
even begin to answer why such changes in personal centers of
energy occurred. There did not need to be any reduction to the
realm of the natural; what was required was only an insistence on a
point of contact with the psychological self and on a definition that
included the natural conditions of the self as part of the conversion
process. There was much to be said about the far side of conversion,

James explained, and his description of the religious self would include a view of it. But first, conversion had to be established on the near and human side, needed to be depicted as a process that was continuous with the self of the pre-converted state.

In addition, for James the experience of conversion always included the activity of the self in bringing about the new, more vital state of being. The will made a deliberate decision to accept and believe in this new center of action. If the self could no longer create beliefs, as it had been able to do in the *Principles*, it nevertheless could in a sense help establish them as permanent. The melancholy of the sick-soul, as James had stated, had seeped beyond the point where any self-enacted restitution was possible; there was no active will to believe. But there remained a willing capacity nonetheless, a passive act of the will, an acquiescence, a "crisis of self-surrender"[62] in which the individual yielded its world of beliefs, gave over its power of definition.

This passive willingness to believe was for James the essential fact of conversion humanly considered; and it was so, moreover, not just because it was fundamental in becoming religious, but because it opened the self to a new way of life and action. Conversion provided the self with a way of re-creation based not on assertion and control but on consent and the putting to rest of assertion.[63] In the extremity of pessimism, where aggressive action was exposed as a diversion and a deceit, there was an action of acknowledgment, a yielding and a sacrifice of the world the self had built for the sake of a wider reality.

> We have used the vague and abstract language of psychology. But since, in any terms, the crisis described is the throwing of our conscious selves upon the mercy of powers which, whatever they may be, are more ideal than we are actually, and make for our redemption, you see why self-surrender has been and always must be regarded as the vital turning-point of the religious life.[64]

Precisely whom it was being yielded to, and to what the power of definition was being given over, remained purposefully ambiguous in James's definition: he defined the wider self as broadly as possible, preferring the "vaguer term subconscious or subliminal" to the usual descriptive phrase "unconscious cerebration." This vagueness, however, was not without its point: as the evidence of conversion gave witness to an active, conditioning self, so also it always had to do with some sort of extramental, infusing power. The imprecision of terms was intended not to preclude the reality of the unseen but to give it a less reductive range.[65]

Toward the close of his lecture on conversion, James made his understanding of the subliminal more precise. Here his psychology took a step forward in its investigations of psychical phenomena. There was, he argued, an "ultra-marginal" consciousness and power, which, while still continuous with the self, could not be made identical to the content of ordinary consciousness. And in conversion it was this "ultra-marginal" that appeared to come into connection with the self's everyday definitions. In its "invasions" and "incursions into the primary consciousness," it gave the self its new focus and center of energy.[66] All of which was to say, even if as yet only provisionally, that conversion was a mutual action of the self and a distinct but not discontinuous "more." Conversion was the consent of the individual to a binding wider than that which the self could assert, and the eruption into consciousness of a new center of life and action.

Conversion, of course, meant nothing apart from its aftermath, for the entity to whom the self turned remained unseen, always a matter of personal overbelief.[67] James thus moved from conversion to the state of saintliness, more specifically to a description of the life led from the new habitual center of personality. It was possible to draw a representative image of the saint, a composite portrait of "universal saintliness." Conversion customarily produced a definite set of changes within the self, alterations of inner conditions and dispositions—a feeling of being in communion and "friendly continuity" with a power greater than the self; a feeling of freedom from the self's former boundaries and an assent to the world now bound by the religious power. These shifts of inner conditions then produced characteristic practical patterns of life and action: devoutness, purity, tenderness, charity, and a degree of worldly asceticism.[68]

The descriptive view of saintliness, in turn, demanded an evaluation of the practical results of the religious encounter. Here James returned to what he again called the common sense method of evaluation, which looked at the general "fitness of saintly activity." Empirically considered, all of the saintly patterns of action seemed prone to excess and extravagance. Like all human products, they were "liable to corruption." "Spiritual excitement" may lead one astray "whenever other interests are too few and the intellect too narrow." There was also a more general propensity of the religious toward base, inhuman action, although these faults of the saintly self were usually attributable to the "unholy entanglements" of the individual with religious institutions: "The basenesses . . . are thus, almost all of them, not chargeable at all to religion proper, but rather to religion's wicked practical partner, the spirit of corporate dominion."[69]

Returning to the primary patterns of saintly activity he had listed earlier, James began what was to be his final delineation of the religious self. Of the four paths of action, devoutness and purity were the least valuable; although they had a certain popular appeal, as ways of action in line with ideals, they were also liable to excess. Particularly when linked with a character that was "masterful and aggressive," they were prone to fanatical patterns of life. And because they tended toward an exclusivism that made the religious self less useful publicly and privately, they needed to be held to a minimum. Neither was "the one thing needful; and it is better that a life should contract many a dirt-mark, then forfeit usefulness in its efforts to remain unspotted."[70]

Conversely, charity and asceticism, those two patterns of action about which the modern age found it "hard to speak without impatience," were evaluated as positive on the whole and, to the extent that they had fallen into disuse, in need of renovation. To be sure, these also had their excesses: charity could "give the universe into the hands of the enemy" by an untempered forgiving; and asceticism, particularly when construed in terms of an older, medieval pattern of action, appeared pathological at best. But both had an essential function in terms of general usefulness, charity creating a prophetic resistance to a world of self-interest, asceticism giving a complementary refusal to take anything but a realistic view.[71]

Charity was not, as the world would have it, merely a way of "preserving the unfit, and breeding parasites and beggars." Instead, it took a stance against existing social and individual relations. The charitable saint provided a perspective that was crucial to society: the saints were "the great torchbearers" of a way of life that was not the way of the world but for that reason needed to be preserved.

James extended charity beyond the realm of individual action to include "the Utopian dreams of social justice in which many contemporary socialists and anarchists indulge." In both its narrow individual and wider social functions, charity acted, at the least, to prevent a kind of "spiritual stagnancy."[72]

Asceticism, for its part, opened a view to, and gave a means of working against, the "element of real wrongness in this world." That is, asceticism stood "for nothing less than the essence of the twice-born philosophy":[73] it actively perceived the tragedy of life and also took an initiative against the evil it saw. Asceticism was not a denial of the world: poverty, privation, the disavowal of honor—all of those things that ran against the grain of modern sensibilities—were not ways of excerpting oneself or of avoiding life's tasks. Instead they were the keys to an existence of genuine engagement, full commitment. And unlike the socially approved paths of militarism, imperial adventure, and material accumulation, asceticism did not have the effect of building self-worth at the expense of society. Above all, asceticism led to real freedom: a freedom from the fear of loss (for it was the reality of loss to which the ascetic had surrendered) and hence a freedom to live in full confrontation with perceived worldly wrongs.

James concluded his discussion of the value of saintliness by comparing the qualities of the saint with those of the "worldly-minded" hero. His model of the self stood in stark contrast to the typical figure of authentic selfhood; it was not yet clear, however, that this model could stand up successfully against its countertype. What James took as his point of contrast was the "masterful, overpowering" hero of a "predaceous military character." To what extent could a positive regard for the saint be maintained in the context of this heroic way of being? Was the saint, in the midst of everyday relations, anything more than "the degenerate par excellence, the man of insufficient vitality?"[74]

James's initial response was to take sides with the heroic model of the self. The saint, given his or her ambivalences, morbidity, and lack of outward power, did appear ill suited for the title of hero, and was by all visible criteria little better than a "sophisticated invalid." "Compared with these beaked and taloned graspers of the world," said James, "saints are herbivorous animals, tame and harmless barnyard poultry." Abstractly considered, of course, the saint seemed the more ideal type; he or she was adapted to the highest society conceivable ("a society in which there should be no aggressiveness, but only sympathy and fairness") in a way that the culturally valorized hero was not.[75]

The point of the evaluation, however, was not ideal but concrete, within the context of the practical and actual, and in judgment upon the adaptability of the saintly self in the light of its "economical relations." Viewed from this perspective the saintly model at first appeared to fare less well: sainthood entailed a higher risk than did a life of aggressive action, and thus a greater potential for failure in the eyes of the world and in one's own eyes as well. "There is, in short, no absoluteness in the excellence of sainthood." There could be no romanticization of the saintly self. "It must be confessed that as far as this world goes, anyone who makes an out and out saint of himself does so at his peril." And the point of greatest peril lay in the possibility of self-betrayal, in the tragic possibility that, without strong mundane interests, saintliness would devour its own aims and efforts. "If [the saint] is not a large enough man, he may appear more insignificant and contemptible, for all his saintliness, than if he had remained a worldling."[76]

Granted this risk, however,—and it was, after all, no more than a repetition of the fact that the self remained bound by the contingency and tragedy of life—the saint far outstripped the hero of aggression in terms of both adaptation and the fulfillment of his or her goals. For the saint was free in the world, rather than, like the hero, only in control of the world at best. Having given over his or her own assertion, the saint could now stand for and against things, could genuinely take a stand. The saints, James concluded, "are like pictures with an atmosphere and background; and placed alongside of them, the strong men of this world and no other seem as dry as sticks, as hard and crude as blocks of stone."[77]

"Let us be saints, then, if we can," was James's last word about his religious and twice-born individual; the practical qualities of a life lived religiously were "indispensable to the world's welfare." For the saint had the chance to give a "leaven of righteousness in the world," a vision and a concrete pattern of life that, as James put it, "would help to set free our generation."[78] Again, there was no guarantee of success; saintliness remained a risk and a wager. And no matter how indispensable the qualities of sainthood might be, they depended on an all-too-fallible judgment in their application. But the wager was worth making, and the effort of response worth taking. That person who fully consented to the reality of the unseen, who brought all of his or her interests into relation with a religious commitment, brought in turn something of "essential sacredness" into the world, "the tender grace," as James put it, echoing his address on Robert Shaw, "not of a day that is dead, but of a day yet to be born somehow."[79]

5

Returning to Experience

It is not how things are in the world that is mystical, but that it exists. There are, indeed, things that cannot be put into words. They make themselves manifest. They are what is mystical.

Ludwig Wittgenstein, *Tractatus*

It might seem odd to leave James in midstream of his *Varieties*, five lectures still to be delivered, and no conclusions clearly drawn. Mysticism, a summary review of the characteristics of the religious life, a word about the relationship between the religious investigations and the worlds of philosophical and theological construction: all of these remained in the balance after the evaluation of saintliness.[1] The twice-born individual, to be sure, had been vindicated; if religion could be of good to human life, it would be by orienting people back within the contingency of things rather than by offering them a means of escape or—and this amounted to the same thing—affirming their assertion of control. But there were other points that needed to be addressed before James could call his work complete, questions about the nature of the experience at the heart of the religious life and, more generally, about the implications of the world of religious experience for the world of life experience.

The lectures on the value of saintliness thus formed a natural stopping place in James's thought; what James said afterward had a different focus and orientation. Gone, for the most part, beyond this point were the evaluative descriptions and typological surveys; the analysis rested less and less on personal and biographical testimonies and explanations. In their place were "spiritual judgments," a series of statements about the varieties of overbeliefs that could be made in light of the previous investigations, the theological outbuildings that could be constructed from the materials and evidence that had been gathered.

Before we move on to James's closing remarks, however, I want to make a comment about the way in which he drew to a close. The conclusions of the *Varieties* were not really conclusions at all, but rather only suggestions and leadings, unfinished sketches of a vision that outran both the space and the scope of the lectures. Religious experience, particularly given James's predilection for the peculiar and extreme, seemed somewhat out of sync with the world of everyday experience; it needed to be grounded, to be described as part of a recognizable world. And the understanding of the object of religious experience needed to be worked through more completely. James's statements seemed to be moving beyond both traditional theistic and monistic conceptions, but in the lectures they remained rooted in their vocabulary and logic. The trouble was that James could not provide all that his prior lectures had asked. As he said over again in his final lectures, his comments were "unsatisfactory from their brevity, and I can only say that I hope to return to the same questions in another book."[2]

Another way to put this would be to say that the religious stories of his lectures broke through the images and the story of the self in the *Principles*. Although James had begun the lectures using that self as his base, by the end he found himself standing face to face with another self of a vastly other world. And again, James did not know how to respond, beyond a general affirmation. Although he had always held that the "lunatic" life of the religious person (and, above all, of the saint) was significant, and increasingly as the nineteenth century wore on became convinced that it was less lunatic than the life of self-assertion burgeoning around him, he had never fully beheld it until now. He did not yet have an explanation of the world in which the religious individual lived, namely, a world of pure experience. It would take some time fully to reformulate his understandings in the light of that world.

Now, what that world was about—a description broached in the conclusions to the Gifford lectures—was constituted very differently from the world of consciousness and the primary processes of the *Principles*. When one stripped away self-assertion and submitted the self, the world appeared more like a web than a mechanical or electrical flow (the metaphors of the *Principles*), a world of conjunctions and relations, filled with connections. Conversion, consent, "cosmic consciousness" as James called it in his lectures on mysticism: the religious self was in a commerce, was not just a self but a-self-with-a-god.[3] The first principle of religious psychology seemed to be the "withness" of the self; as James explained it, the religious individual "becomes conscious that his higher part is coterminous and continuous with a MORE of the same quality, which is operative in the universe outside of him, and which he can keep in working touch with.[4]

That world of conjunctions seemed to offer a different kind of cure for the self from the one James had offered in his work up to this point. Again, James wanted such an alternative, having seen how the self in the *Principles* had turned out. But he did not know quite what to do with it yet. For James's empiricism had held him, if with a strain, to the conclusion that nothing that was immediately given could go beyond itself. That was why self-assertion had made sense as a cure: because the self was always singular, one had to make do and re-create on one's own. Here now was a self, however, for whom self-transcendence was an everyday occurrence, whose life was with a "more," and hence who lived more than his or her own life, and whose narrative was never just his or her own.

The chance for salvation, to use the phraseology that James employed in his final lectures,[5] thus lay not only with the self but with the self with someone more. It resided in relation, in acceptance rather than re-creation, in letting go instead of taking control. Simply put, it meant going with experience rather than trying to legislate and transform it. That gave the self the freedom to be honest about one's sick-souled human state. It also allowed the freedom to be open to help, that is, to be free for another instead of just for oneself.

When James ended his Gifford lectures, he did so with a new psychological world before him, a world that was more genuinely constructive, for it was built along with many, was a joint effort. He had come up with what amounted to a new psychological perspective. As he wrote in a letter to François Pillon, he had come face to face with a "radical empiricism, a pluralism, a tychism, which represents order as being gradually won and always in the making."[6] But that world still needed to be filled out. James was in the position of "a man who must set his back against an open door quickly if he does not wish to see it closed and locked."[7] The filling out of that new world constituted the remaining work of James's career.

It has been said that James became a philosopher after the *Varieties*, which is to the point if by it is meant that he tried to explain the underpinnings of his re-visioned work, but misleading if it is taken to indicate a turn away from prior projects and from popular concerns and interests. James still wanted his lectures and writings to be responsive to a generation that craved "more of the temperament of life in its philosophy, even though it were at some cost of logical rigor and formal purity."[8] In turn, he continued to see his work as a description and re-visioning of the life of his culture and class. What makes the most sense of James's later work is to see it as part and parcel of an overall project. James continued to be a religious psychologist. Indeed, his last writings were a rewriting of the self and the psychological world of the *Principles* in the light of the self and the religious world of the *Varieties*.

This continuation and re-viewing was apparent in James's *Essays in Radical Experience*, a series of articles originally published in the *Journal of Philosophy, Psychology, and Scientific Methods.*[9] Here James defined and described his view of the world: an "evolution of the psychical from the bosom of the physical," an "experience chaos" burgeoning out into actions, reactions, and gradually, partially realized ideals.[10] The articles were essays in the true sense of the word, attempts that went only part of the way toward reaching their ends. They attempted to provide sketches of the nonfoundational world of the early psychology in the light of the cluster of problems about experience that had been raised by the Gifford lectures.

"Does consciousness exist?" James asked in his opening article on radical empiricism. His rather abrupt reply was that there was "no aboriginal stuff or quality of being, contrasted with that of which material objects are made, out of which our thoughts of them are made." Consciousness was the name of a "non-entity." Thoughts performed a function (knowing) in experience, "for the performance of which this quality of being is invoked."[11] But the usual duality between consciousness and content was not a real one;

there was no truth to the assertion of two separate substances, thoughts, and things.

What there was—and here James offered the first lines of his new vision—was simply a world of pure experience, a concatenation of "simple thats" which, in different conjunctions with one another, formed what common sense called the real and ideal worlds, the realms of thoughts and extensions, knowers and knowns, subjects and objects.[12] James placed all of the possible worlds of belief into the flow of experience; everything from physical facts to dreamed idols of imagination were transformed into functions of experience, the upshot of varied and varying groupings and contexts.[13] Using the image of a quantity of paint to make his point, James explained:

> In a pot in a paint-shop . . . it serves in its entirety as so much saleable matter. Spread on a canvas, with other paints around it, it represents, on the contrary, a feature in a picture. . . . Just so, I maintain, does a given undivided portion of experience, taken in one context of associates, play the part of a knower, of a state of mind, of consciousness; while in a different context the same undivided bit of experience plays the part of a thing known, of an objective content.[14]

All of this may seem to be a simple repetition of the fundamental principles of James's psychology, specifically of his insistence in the *Principles* that everything be regarded as having an organic base. And it is such a repetition, save for the fact that it replaced the conscious self, which in the *Principles* has slipped gradually over and above the primary processes, fully back into the organic flow. In the *Principles* James had worked with the image of a theater of possibility, a stage of experience upon which the self performed its interested and aspiring acts. In the *Essays* the same image was applied, but with an important modification: once again there was the theater and the actors, but now with all but functional distinctions discarded. Action—the selecting and sustaining of certain portions of the stream of thought—and the ground of action—the flowing stream or the theater of possibilities—had been merged. Where in the *Principles* there had finally still been two things together that produced a drama, now there was nothing but the drama itself, a single sheet of action and play. "Im Anfang war die

Tat,"[15] James said, quoting from Goethe: in the beginning was the deed, or fact.

This modification in the image of the self was not a difficult one for James to make. He had moved back and forth on the issue of dualism in his psychological portrait, many times emphasizing the sole activity of the "passing thought"[16] as closer to the truth than descriptions that held to some sort of a separative self. "Does Consciousness Exist?" simply took that emphasis and made it definite. It cleared James's psychology, once and for all, of any notion of a detached, observing being above and beyond the flux of things. In turn, it allowed for a new view of the relations among things in experience, one that had no need for the assertions of the old psychological self.

James's second essay, "A World of Pure Experience," showed the first fruits of that modification; it dealt directly with the issues of conjunctive relations raised in the *Varieties*, arguing not only that there needed to be no duality between subject and object, but also that within the experiential flow all relations, from mere "and-ness" to full communion, could be found.[17] James opened this second essay with a slight redefinition of his radical empiricism: what he wanted to express was a " mosaic philosophy," a description of a world in which "experience itself, taken at large, can grow by its edges." That is, the relations of conjunction and disjunction, like the thoughts and things discussed in the initial essay, were functions of experience: "In radical empiricism there is no bedding, it is as if the pieces clung together by their edges, the transitions experienced between them forming their cement. . . . That one moment [of experience] proliferates into the next by transitions which, whether conjunctive or disjunctive, continue the experiential tissue, can not, I contend, be denied."[18]

What James accomplished in this second essay was the inclusion of the religious understanding that experience goes beyond itself, and that it does so without having to resort to any transcendent realm. The world of immediate facts did not have to be a "congeries of solipsisms" waiting for some "I" or God to gather them up and remake them into a world of discourse and meaningful life. Within the pulses of experience were realized all the movements that had formerly been within the purview of the Absolute. "With transition and prospect thus enthroned in pure experience," James wrote, "it is impossible to subscribe to the idealism of the English school."[19]

Far more important, from the perspective of James's vision, was the fact that the essay made an addition to his image, a principle of organic growth, of evolution and adaptability in the heart of experience. Experience now grew and transformed all by itself. Whereas the principle of the early psychology had been that "thought goes on," now that principle needed to be restated in terms of the "withness" that the *Varieties* had discovered. "The gist of the matter is always the same," James put it in a later, summary article; "something ever goes indissolubly with something else."[20] Stated in terms of the image of a drama, the actions performed now constituted a story, or at least a constant interplay. "Life is in the transitions as much as in the terms connected," James wrote; "often, indeed, it seems to be there more emphatically, as if our spurts and sallies forward were the real firing-line of the battle, were like the thin line of flame advancing across the dry autumnal field which the farmer proceeds to burn."[21]

Finally, this second article, and the two following essays continued this theme,[22] provided James's vision with a principle of intimacy, again drawn from the religious investigations. Seen from within the experiential stream and in terms of the structure of the experienced world, all experience belonged together: one way or another, and even in radical disjunction, everything was fluid. As James stated in "The Thing and Its Relations": "The continuities and the discontinuities are absolutely coordinate matters of immediate feeling. . . . They, too, compenetrate harmoniously."[23] To talk about relations in experience, and of whatever sort, was to talk of a world that was all of a piece, internally held together. The gathering self of the *Principles* was not just wrongheaded but wrapped up in relations of deceit. What James had called the "marginal" in the Gifford lectures, here the "relations," were in control: transforming action was properly only a part of the drama in the relational play.

What James had given away in these essays was as important as what he had provided. If he had drawn an image of a world filled with transition and possibility and prospect, he had taken away the transforming agent, the self that had made that world a history, a world that amounted to something. Thus far James's new world of experience was merely a neutral world composed of mere "thats." James admitted as much when he said that the world he had described could be seen as "a universe of experiences in which the only alternative between neighbors would be either physical interaction or complete inertness. In such a world the mental or physical status of any piece of experience would be unequivocal."[24] The point of the *Principles*, however, and of James's work overall, had been to give a world of worths and meanings, something more than a flat, nonfoundational flow. What was there of value and qualification in this new world of experience? More simply put, what was it all worth?

In "The Place of Affectional Facts in a World of Pure Experience," James discussed the subworld of experienced "appreciations," all of that which provided interest, importance, and emotionality to life.[25] And he did it, again, without going beyond the limits of his now radically nonfoundational world, a world based only on experience. Within the tissue of experience, James explained, there were not only things and their relations but also affective experiences, "our pleasures and pains, our loves and fears and angers, the beauty, comicality, importance or preciousness of certain objects and situations." The way in which this list was compiled was telling; it explained the peculiarity of these kinds of relations. Feelings of affection were "amphibious"; they floated from place to place without a fixed reference. Sometimes they seemed to be "our" appreciations, a subjective addition to the physical facts (as in our hatred of someone). At other times the experience ran the other way, and the object, the "someone," really was hateful.[26]

Such a view of affections cut against the usual psychological grain. In affections, it was customary to argue, there appeared to be something inimical to physical objects, or a set of facts that existed in consciousness only. All those feelings of worth that James had listed were normally taken to be "a great realm of experience intuitively recognized as spiritual," that is to say, made of consciousness only and thus different in nature from the "space-filling kind of being which is enjoyed by physical objects."[27]

James went back to his *Principles*, specifically to his theory of emotions, to overcome this objection.[28] There, emotions were shown to be simultaneously affections of the body, whatever else they might also be. That was enough to break the intuitive spell. In his present essay he simply extended his earlier theory, explaining that not only emotions but the whole range of affections remained ambiguous and equivocal. "With the affectional experiences which we are considering, the relatively pure conditions last," said James. By the "pure" condition he meant the simple state of being "that." "In practical life no urgent need has yet arisen for deciding whether to treat [the affections] as rigorously mental or as rigorously physical facts."[29]

So James now had his world of experience as a world of worths, a landscape with inherent value rather than just a picture that could be evaluated. To revert once again to the image of the drama, there was now a play almost in the full sense of the word, a reading instead of only a recitation, no longer a monotonous movement from line to line but a rendering full of phrasing and accents, expression and emotion. But it was still not quite a drama in the most complete sense, or at least not in the sense that James wanted it to be, for it remained without any particular purpose; it had no line of action.

James took up the task of filling out his vision in his 1904 presidential address before the American Psychological Association.[30] He took as his theme the "experience of activity," and began by defining his object. "Bare activity," the experience of something going on, was defined easily within experience, but not fully enough. It offered only a "picture gallery," and not, as James wanted, a sense of full-blooded life. The kind of activity that fit James's intention was that which was experienced as "work," directed activity pushing forward toward a goal, in a word the kind of activity that, in the *Principles*, had belonged to the asserting self.[31] Here was a case, once again, of James's seeking to satisfy the common sense craving for the termperament of life, for the sense of life as an active endeavor.

What James found in experience were "activity-situations,"[32] complexes of experience best expressed as feelings of tendency. Here, at a stroke, were all the elements to give dramatic shape to his world view. What was meant by tendency, after all, was effort and will, resistance and overcoming. All of these could be understood in terms of relations instead of self-assertions. Within experience could be found whatever anyone might possibly mean by activity:

> *There* is complete activity in its original and first intention. What it is known as is what there appears. The experiencer of such a

situation possesses all that the idea contains. He feels the tendency, the obstacle, the will, the triumph, or the passive giving up,
just as he feels the time, the space, the swiftness or intensity, the
movement, the weight and color, the pain and pleasure, the
complexity or whatever remaining characters the situation may
involve. He goes through all that ever can be imagined where
activity is supposed.[33]

This description of the sense of life that was found in experience
did not yet answer the larger question of activity: "What propels
experience *uberhaupt* into being?"[34] It was the problem of causality
that lay at the heart of this question, or better the problem of
creation. Feelings of activity, or so went the usual complaint, were
simply copies, shadows of a more real, original fact. Real activities
were those that "really make things be, without which the things are
not, and with which they are there."[35]

Once again, James's reply was straightforward: the criticism
rested on an unnecessary split between appearance and reality;
ordinary, naive experience delivered "the whole butt and being"[36]
of activity. Where, within experience, effectuation was located,
"which things are the true causal agents there, and of what the more
remote effects consist,"[37] James did not answer directly. He merely
specified the general ways in which these questions could be answered on empirical terms. But that did not deny his point that
cause and creation were a matter of experience and not of something behind or above it. Neither was more sublime than anything
else; they both lived, as James put it, "in the dirt of the world." The
healthy thing for philosophy to do, he concluded, "is to leave off
grubbing underground for what effects effectuation, or what makes
action act, and to try to solve the concrete questions."[38]

With the experience of activity worked out, James had expressed
the rudiments of his re-visioned psychology fairly completely. He
had developed, in its basics, an alternative to the flat, materialistic
vision against which he had struggled throughout his career, as well
as an alternative to the idealist, romanticist vision of the turn of the
century. Much of what he argued in these essays was simply a
restatement of the arguments in the *Principles* for a world without
any ultimate grounding, a world of personal experience. But the
center of that world, the human individual, had shifted, or better
put, had been re-placed.

As a result of that re-placement, the point of James's psychology was also different from what it had been fifteen years before. Now there was a full-blown, primary world of social relations, of actors acting in concert to bring about a play in which everyone had his or her part. Individuals remained, to be sure, as felt centers of experience, and their contributions were crucial. As James put it, "A little thrombus in a statesman's meningeal artery will throw an empire out of gear." But the individual was now no longer the original fact; the gallery of individual portraits, each with its own self-determined narrative, had been converted into the free play of experience. What now was original was the interplay and commerce between the actors in the drama; more than that, it was the work that the drama effected. "The worth and interest of the world," James concluded in "The Experience of Activity," "consists not in its elements, be these elements things, or be they the conjunctions of things; it exists rather in the dramatic outcome in the whole process, and in the meaning of the succession stages which the elements work out."[39]

The new psychological world that James had portrayed seemed to leave some things untold: tragedy and failure, of which he had made so much in the rest of his work, were absent; the "truth" of the experiential flow seemed to be simply a matter of the ways in which various "bits of pure experience" adapted and wedded themselves to one another. James had given only a partial expression of the temperament of life, a problem inherent in the point of view taken in the *Essays*, where everything was portrayed only in terms of the present tense; the world was looked at only by way of things as they are, only functionally and in the abstract.

What was needed were answers to questions about the future. Was there a counterclaim to the notion that "the sun sets in a sea of disappointment"?[40] More generally, could James's world of experience be regarded as moving toward some particular end? "The really vital question for us all," James wrote in his lectures on pragmatism, "is what is this world going to be? What is life eventually to make of itself?"[41] Was there promise as well as possibility in the empiricist vision, and where promise saw fit to fail, was there reason to believe in a possible deliverance?

James took up these questions in his last two major works, *Pragmatism* and *A Pluralistic Universe*. The lectures on pragmatism focused specifically on the understanding of promise and futurity; they were an attempt to ascertain what validity there might be to claims that the world was not merely running down or around and around. *A Pluralistic Universe* summed up the world of promise of the lectures on pragmatism, and added to them a description of the varieties of powers at work in the world, making good or not on the promises that had been defined. Both of these works were attempts to bring into James's re-visioned psychology all of the religious points and personalities that had been suggested in the Gifford lectures. Pragmatism was a "harmonizer of empiricist ways of thinking with the more religious demands of human beings."[42] And James's pluralistic universe was a direct answer to the central religious question of what the world was bound to be.

Much has been said already, both explicitly and implicitly, about James's pragmatism, or at least about its nature and status as a method of investigation. A summary statement here will suffice. The pragmatic method, simply put, was a way to deal with cognitive claims on a nonfoundational basis, to inquire about the meaning and truth of a particular holding, or to settle a dispute between rival claims, by placing them back in the stream of experience and seeing how they were different:

> The pragmatic method is to try to interpret each notion by tracing its practical consequences. What difference would it practically make to anyone if this notion rather than that notion were true? If no practical difference whatever can be traced, then the alternatives mean practically the same thing, and all dispute is idle.[43]

The purpose of the pragmatic method, in turn, was to break the spell of verbal arguments, to deconstruct the notion that there was a separate realm of words[44]—and therefore of stories and meanings— apart from the rest of experience. Experience was prospective in and of itself: meanings, words, languages, ideas were all *of* experience. Put slightly differently, all of these were experience's leadings, for example, how experience meant. This is what James intended when he linked pragmatism to practical outcomes: not that ideas and meanings are creations apart from experience that enter into experience and break it up (and hence should be evaluated on the basis of how they break things up), but rather that they are experiences breaking out, and should be judged practically, in terms of what experience did or was up to or about. As James led the self back to experience in the *Essays*, so here he did the same with language and meanings. Truth was returned to the heart of things, to being part of what experience was.

As these comments make clear, pragmatism was more than just a method; it was the expression of James's new psychological world, now with an eye on that world's forward-moving flow. *Pragma*, the Greek word meaning practice or action, was no different from the understanding that experience was concatenated, really growing, moving toward a next, practical outcome. "We live forwards," said James, quoting from Kierkegaard.[45] Pragmatism was just the explication of that forward movement. Put another way, it was radical empiricism in the optative mood, an evaluation of experience in the making, as it was coming to be.

Pragmatism also stood as a translation of James's radical empiricist world into everyday terms. Conceptual and physical relations and complexes, experiential tendencies, felt centers overcoming and succumbing to resistance in an experiential field could now be recast into everyday language, depicted in terms of a practical, socially constructed world of successes and tragedies, real frustrations and achievements. Functions in experience, seen now from the perspective of their practice, suddenly came alive; they were no longer thoughts and things but people and places, projects and dreams. With language embedded once more in the world, experience attained that full sense of life that was missing in the *Essays*.[46]

What was offered by a pragmatic view of the world, James contended, was a way of evaluating that ran between the usual choices of rationalism and materialism, the former of which "derealized" the world of everyday fact by forcing it into a correspondence with an absolute, the latter of which left it realized but with a purposeless, enervated realization. Neither rationalism nor materialism could yield a world with any prospective value or promise. The point was obvious according to the materialist way of thinking: there, real possibility was, quite simply, impossible. And the same point could be made about the rationalist perspective: its possibility came with such a guarantee that it lapsed into certainty. Rationalism, James argued, was "no explanation of our concrete universe, it is another thing altogether, a substitute for it, a remedy, a way of escape."[47]

James built his middle way by compromise, the first step of which was to defuse certain traditional prejudices that surrounded the opposing sides. Materialism, or "crude naturalism," would have to relinquish its prejudice, particularly against religious claims; more generally, it would have to allow for rationalistic positions where they were warranted by the facts. Rationalism, or "vicious intellectualism," had in turn to agree that its reasons were simply aspects of the experienced world without any special privilege; more to the point, it had to forsake the desire, which ran against the experienced facts, to reduce the world to an ordered, well-mannered flow. James wrote:

> Refinement is what characterizes our intellectualistic philosophies. But I ask you in all seriousness to look abroad on this colossal universe of concrete facts, on their awful bewilderment, their surprises and cruelties, on the wildness which they show, and then to tell me whether "refined" is the one inevitable descriptive adjective that springs to your lips.[48]

With privileges and prejudices abolished, and with a common understanding that there could be resolutions to differences only when those resolutions were "realized in *rebus*,"[49] there could be discussion rather than simple conflict; options could be evaluated; the pragmatist perspective could be constructed. James reviewed four general dilemmas as he set his task: on the unity and plurality of the world, the meaning of truth, the possibility of creative action, and the likelihood of deliverance or salvation. The resolution of each of these would provide the primary elements of the prospective view of the radical empiricist world.

Turning first to the issue of pluralism versus monism, James argued that experience yielded a world neither of one nor of many. Returning to his understanding that experience contained both disjunctions and conjunctions, he explained that pragmatism had, finally, to "abjure absolute monism and absolute pluralism." Stated positively, the world appeared as a chaos and an order, with various and frequently competing causes, concerns, and ends. Sometimes, to be sure, there were unities in things: "Things tell a story. Their parts hang together so as to work out a climax. They play into each other's hands expressively." But the unities were never complete.

"The world appears," James concluded, refining his image from the *Essays*, "as something more epic than dramatic."[50]

As was the case with the many and the one, so it was with the question of the meaning of truth. The world did not appear blind, utterly without a sense of truth. Ideas did sometimes bear themselves out and prove to be worthwhile leadings. At the same time, however, there was no such thing as truth once and for all, truth as an inert static relation: "The truth; what a perfect idol of the rationalistic mind! . . . The question 'what is the truth?' is no real question." For pragmatism, the first point about truth was that it was ambiguous; there would always be "later revelations of the story." To talk of truth was to talk about workable strategies, ideas in their working-out. Thus it was to talk about these only penultimately, never finally or for good. Truths, for James, were always boiling over into new truths and falsehoods. "Truth grafts itself on previous truth, modifying it in the process, just as idiom grafts itself on previous idiom, and law on previous law."[51]

It was only a short step from the notion of truth as ambiguous to the notion that truth is constructed, more generally that the world is malleable. In "Pragmatism and Humanism" James made the move. Rationalism viewed the world as already made up in advance, complete for all eternity. Its universe was "absolutely secure," with little but a show of novelty and change. The world of experience, however, had not and did not need a "doctrinaire and authoritative complexion." It was a concatenation of "maybes" and not a single "must." It appeared as a work always unfinished, without any "edition de luxe, eternally complete," hovering behind it.[52] Finally, it could be changed from what it formerly was; to be unfinished, after all, meant to be open to the not-yet and the new. What existed really could come to something different, and by our constructive work.

This did not mean that pragmatism rejected outright the rationalist vision; when it came to the question of the final form of all the changes that were afoot, the rationalists had a point to make. Here James differentiated himself from others within the pragmatist fold. Pragmatism, he explained, was perhaps anarchistic but not radically so; there might be bindings beyond the world's finite ties. Indeed, the hypothesis of a "more" to life, exerting a wider binding power and adding to the world's novelties and changes, was a live option, one that arose from and led back to sensible realities. To reject the belief in a God quite literally made no sense. A God of some sort was a fact among all the others, even if it pointed to something broader than the facts of everyday experience.[53]

To say all of this, however (and James spent the remainder of "Pragmatism and Religion" explaining the point), did not signal an adoption of the rationalist's hypothesis of a foundational world. In the first place, pragmatism altered the orientation of the hypothesis: it was not a matter of looking backward, a belief in the rational unity of things, but rather an anticipation of things to come, a belief in "their possible empirical unification." Concomitantly, the truth of the hypothesis was not that there was an Absolute before the fact, but rather only an ultimate in the midst of things. Finally, the point of the hypothesis was that "the world may be saved," instead of the usual rationalistic insistence that "the world must and shall be saved."[54]

Pragmatism, James concluded, promoted a "melioristic" doctrine, a recognition of possibilities that were live but still only contingently grounded: "Some conditions of the world's salvation are actually existent, and [pragmatism] cannot possibly close her eyes to this fact: and should the residual conditions come, salvation would become an accomplished reality." This position was clearly not a resort to a rational universe or a foundational world beyond the empirical facts; it was an explanation of the world of experience, the "workshop of being," in which the "social scheme of cooperative work" actually added its cumulative strokes. Neither was it a way of bringing in an all-healing power of divinity; for James, the theological pragma that proved most useful was of a co-creative God or gods "in the midst of all the shapers of the great world's fate."[55]

Meliorism had its darker side as well; if it was not nihilistic as with the materialists, neither was it optimistic as with the rationalists. The prospects of salvation and unification remained always "uncertified possibilities," matters of trust and faith. Disintegration was as much at work in the world as integration; "ineluctable noes and losses" formed a part of things along with the yesses and gains. The world, as James put it, was "drastic" at least in part, tragic in that some things were just an empty waste and fraud. Genuine pragmatists, James concluded, were again of the sick-souled type, like "those puritans who answered yes to the question: Are you willing to be damned for God's glory?" They recognized that some events were simply losses left unredeemed.[56]

The pragmatic world of promise that James defined remained, then, a world of chances: not the dead chance of the materialist, for whom chance finally meant nothing at all; and not the certain chance of the rationalist, for whom chance was something that could be grounded; but rather an open, intrinsic chance, a working chance for change. And it was a world of promise that had been radicalized, that was set flush against the fact that all promises could be broken, but did not have to be. In sum, the world of promise was a world of freedom, a free promise given without a covenant of assurance or a contract, given for nothing. When one looked forward in the radical empiricist world, one found freedom. This was the new element that James's *Pragmatism* added to his re-visioned psychology: freedom as *the* pragma of experience.

As the world of promise remained a world of chances, so it stayed an arena of practice, an evolving world of work some of which reached its end, some of which fell behind, much of which came to nothing at all. There may be a final unification, James concluded, but not without its cost. If the world were to be saved, it would be in the twice-born way, tragic and comic at once. Let the hypothesis of salvation be a live one, James argued at the end of his lectures, but recognize the kind of promise that it entails. There are no guarantees that the mission will be successful; at best it will be an epic human drama. James wrote: "I offer you the chance of taking part in such a world. Its safety, you see, is unwarranted. It is a real adventure, with real danger, yet it may win through. It is a social scheme of cooperative work genuinely to be done. Will you join the procession? Will you trust yourself and trust the other agents enough to face the risk?"[57]

We have run inadvertently into a story of sorts, one that probably should not be taken too literally, but which needs to be mentioned, at least in brief. And that story is that James's later works, those that came out of the conversion of the *Varieties*, are running parallel to the major portions of his work in the *Principles*. As in the initial section of the *Principles*, where James deconstructed the self into its primary processes, so, in a re-visioned form, the *Essays* deconstruct the self again (this time in terms of pure experience). And as in the second section of the psychology, where James described the personal aspect of self-consciousness, so do the lectures on pragmatism redescribe that personal aspect as a world of personal value and worth (meaning, truth, and so on as experience). If the story runs true to form, and in this case it seems to, *A Pluralistic Universe* should re-vision the final section of the *Principles*, where James turned his theater into a stage with an asserted act. This is in fact what the Hibbert lectures did: they described the world of experience in its aspect of powers; they re-visioned the psychology by redescribing power as cooperation rather than as an individual possession, as submission and mutuality.

The topic of these lectures, then, was not simply pluralism as such but the way in which powers and the empowerment to work could be explained from a pluralistic perspective. James's vision was of a world bound up by cooperative efforts both human and more than human. There were, for James, powers of all sorts afoot in the world, breaking through the provisional and sometimes creating real reconciliations and unifications. Experience, now filled with meanings and narratives, was not just an act but alive: it was the "lunatic" vision of the *Varieties* described in terms of what it was to undergo that vision; it was a "panpsychism," a world in which everything was in relation.

Stated another way, the topic of *A Pluralistic Universe* was the religious nature of the world of pure experience, what were the powers of experience, understood in the sense of what experience was bound to be. Narrowly construed, the lectures were about humans and the gods, and the kinds of bindings that constituted their relations. More broadly, the lectures concerned the story or play that experience was about, how it was bound to turn out, what its religious dimension was overall. James simply was trying to describe experience from the perspective of ultimacy, but in terms of his radical empiricism.

He explained his topic by juxtaposing his own description with the monistic description, that is, the description that gave conceptual sense to the romantic vision. By monism James meant the ascription of an "all-form" to things, of an absolute God and creator of the world and of a single, final narrative already made up in advance. Empiricism and pluralism were not forms of monism in disguise. They held, in terms of common sense, that the temperament of life was not one of surety. It did not have a single story, or at least not one based on experience. There could be no hypothesis of what James called a "metaphysical monster" of an Absolute in the pluralistic vision: such a hypothesis was not wrong but impossible in practice. An overarching story just could not be discerned: "What boots it to tell me that the absolute way is the true way, and to exhort me, as Emerson says, to lift mine eyes up to its style, and manners of the sky, if the feat is impossible by definition? I am finite once and for all, and all the categories of my sympathy are knit up with the finite world as such."[58]

The argument that the monistic description was a will to believe with only false relations to experience took up the bulk of James's first three lectures. They cleared the air of any ambiguities that might have resulted from his avowal of a religious dimension to life. Monism and pluralism were aligned only to the extent that both held to a "social relation" between the world and its God; both stood opposed to nontheistic materialism, which, as James said, he needed not discuss again, and to traditional theisms, which left a gap of foreignness, an inorganic tie between divinity and what was usually its creation. James gave theism a brief treatment; it was, after all, at least a spiritual vision of the cosmos. But it was spiritualism without any definable spiritual ties: the theistic God and the creature were "*toto genere* distinct." Theism's God provided at best only a unilateral relation. "His action can affect us," James explained, "but he can never be affected by our reaction. Of course in common men's religion the relation is believed to be social, but that is only one of the differences between religion and theology."[59]

Having raised the charge of foreignness and lack of relation, James then turned it on the monistic hypothesis. Despite monism's pantheistic claims to intimacy—and by pantheism James meant only a general notion of sociality—monism, like theism, finally left the world radically split in two. To be sure, monism made the absolute and the world one fact; everything was revised upward, into the unity of a whole of which we are the parts. Practically and formally, however, the community of this whole and its parts broke down: things that were true of the world as finite, for example, its ignorances and evils, were not true of the world taken infinitely. There was a discrepancy, and a radical one, between the relative view from below and the absolute view from above, and, as James had argued over and again, points of view were not just trifling matters. We have a history and the Absolute does not. We move step by step; the Absolute, if it could be said to move at all, steps all at once and once for all. "Let us imitate the All, said the original prospectus of the admirable Chicago quarterly called the *Monist*. As if we could, either in thought or conduct! We are invincibly parts, let us talk as we will, and must always apprehend the absolute as if it were a foreign being."[60]

More had to be said about monism than just this complaint about foreignness. Arguers for the absolute unity of things, after all, insisted that any apparent discrepancies and bifurcations were overcome by an intimacy of reason: the Absolute was not a hypothesis but a presupposition. "The primal whole," James explained, "which is their vision must be there not only as a fact but as a logical necessity."[61] It was the bare minimum that could be thought of; without it there could be absolutely nothing. To talk about unification, the monists argued, or about some kind of real independence of things was just nonsense. Admit even a degree of independence, and you would be thrown into an irrational infinite regress. Either the world was one or it was many; a plural universe had no logic to it. The radical empiricist vision of "eaches" and of partial rationalities was a world not of real chances but of mere randomness, chaos plain and simple.

James's reply was straightforward: all of this was just a form of "vicious intellectualism," a way of arguing that refused to allow for qualifications, even when they could be shown in fact. "As well might you contend," he countered, "that a person whom you have once called an equestrian is thereby forever made unable to walk on his own feet."[62] Definitions and names were not, as the monists would have it, exclusive, but rather only particular; their descriptions did not rule out but only, as it were, ruled in. Monism could not accept the truth about the word *some*, James explained, which lay at the heart of the empiricist vision: "Absolutism, on its side, seems to hold that 'some' is a category ruinously infected with self-contradictoriness, and that the only categories universally consistent and therefore pertinent to reality are 'all' and 'none.'"[63]

The monistic vision of an incontrovertible truth, of an eternal "must" that could admit of no "maybes," reached its height, according to James, in the philosophy of Hegel, and if James were to clear the boards of monism, he would have to reckon with Hegel's explanation. The Hegelian vision, James argued, was essentially twofold, an understanding that the things of the world are dialectical, and a perception that reason is all-embracing. The first part of the vision, which was simply a description of the world as a "dogging of everything by its negative," was "not only harmless but accurate,"[64] simply another way of taking the empiricist world view. When it was linked to the second half of the vision, however,—that is, when dialectic was converted into an ineluctable and all-binding logic—then it lost its empiricist orientation, succumbed to the monistic view that "in the end nothing less than the whole of everything can be the truth of anything at all."[65]

Hegel's predilection for the conceptual over the sensational, then—what amounted to his "method of double negation"—was the point of failure in his world view, a case of vicious intellectualism in extremis: "Every idea of a finite thing is of course a concept of *that* thing and not a concept of anything else. But Hegel treats this not being a concept of anything else as if it were equivalent to the concept of anything else not being, or in other words as if it were a denial or negation of everything else."[66] With this redefinition of things the conceptual pulse of the dialectic commenced, and continued until it reached the point of Hegel's absolute idea or mind. But it did so at the expense of the first part of Hegel's vision, casting all of the oppositions, the particular tensions of things, into a realm of illusion. "The true knowledge of God begins," James quoted from Hegel's *Logic*, "when we know that things, as they immediately are, have no truth."[67]

The end of Hegel's system, like all monistic systems, was to answer the world's complexities by escaping them. It allowed for a "moral holiday," as James put it, from the strenuousness of everyday life; but it gave little by way of an explanation of things as they were experienced. As a hypothesis the absolute of Hegelian conception proved useless: "You cannot enter the phenomenal world with the notion of it in your grasp, and name beforehand any detail which you are likely to meet there."[68] Like all other notions of the absolute, James concluded, returning to his argument in *Pragmatism*, Hegel's grand conception functioned only retrospectively. And it brought in its wake a host of insoluble riddles, above all a problem of evil the absolute answer to which was inadequate and offensive: "The sum of it all is that the absolute is not forced on our belief by logic, that it involves features of irrationality peculiar to itself, and that a thinker to whom it does not come as an 'immediate certainty' is in no way bound to treat it as anything but an emotionally rather sublime hypothesis."[69]

"Let the Absolute bury the Absolute," James concluded; monism was "but the old story, of a useful practice first becoming a method, then a habit, and finally a tyranny that defeats the end it was used for."[70] It was to be hoped that his arguments against the absolutistic hypothesis had broken the hegemony of the monist claims, and that monism's vicious intellectualism, its privative use of concepts, and its belief that truth was nearer when life was abstracted no longer needed to be given so much sway. Above all, it was to be hoped that good reasons had been given to forswear the backward-and upward-looking glance as the proper way to find life's meaning.

There was, however, a cost to forgetting and turning away: idols of considerable power would be buried along with the Absolute. To take up the pluralistic hypothesis, really to go "behind the conceptual function . . . to the more primitive flux," was to be religiously overturned. It meant putting oneself through an "inner crisis or catastrophe"; it entailed a loss of security and of certain conceptual defenses. The romantic, idealist tradition, which held fixity and abstraction to be the regnant realms, was painful to lose, for it amounted to a loss of control: "We are so subject to the philosophic tradition which treats logos or discursive thought generally as the sole avenue to truth, that to fall back on raw unverbalized life as more of a revealer . . . comes very hard. It is putting off our proud maturity of mind and becoming as foolish little children in the eyes of reason."[71]

Above all, to walk away from monism, and toward the pluralistic vision was to be humbled. Here James marked a change not only of focus in his lectures but also in his mode of expression. One now had to give up the detached and observational view of the world that looked on life from a distance. The pluralist, said James, had to "lie flat on [his] belly in the middle of experience"; pluralism's ways were not the ways of static review but rather of active, participatory insight. Philosophical explanation thus had to be forsworn: "As long as talk continues talking, intellectualism remains in undisturbed possession of the field. The return to life can't come about by talking. It is an act; to make you return to life I must set an example for your imitation, I must deafen you to talk."[72]

Six more lectures remained to be given. With each succeeding one James relied more and more on description and less on explanation; his points were made quite literally by pointing rather than by proving. What James was after now was a final show of the pluralistic universe at work, en route to its kind of unification and reconciliation. The task was to try to exhibit the active compoundings and continuities in things, that ineluctable impulse of consent. But this would have to be done by appeal and not by demonstration; it had to be a matter of conviction and not merely of being convinced.

James set about his task by giving credit to those from whom he had gained his own empiricist convictions. In a lecture on Gustav Fechner, James reintroduced the understanding, implicit in his argument against the monists, that there was such a thing as the compounding of consciousness, that is, "that states of consciousness, so called, can separate and combine themselves freely, and keep their own identity unchanged while forming parts of simultaneous fields of experience of wider scope."[73] Fechner, with his "daylight view" of the world, which saw that "the abstract lived in the concrete," made James recognize that "the more inclusive forms of consciousness are in part constituted by the more limited forms." If James did not follow Fechner to his absolutistic end, he did take away from him a panpsychic vision, one which he then had to square with his empiricism and pluralism. And Fechner did one thing more: he led James to the theoretical impasse where logic had to be abandoned, where the frank admission had to be made that, given the facts of consciousness interflowing, reality—"where things happen"—was nonrational in its constitution.[74]

If Fechner set the terms and the dilemma of James's vision, Henri Bergson brought on the catastrophe. Bergson, as James put it, pushed for an intuitive view of the "passing moment," for a look at life "in the intervals." He called for a perspective in which change rather than fixity was the "nobler," and in which particular experiences were given status over "universal conceptions." All of this, James explained, broke the sway of the logic of identity once and for all; from Bergson, James could begin to see the conjunctive relations in experience, the world of conflux that had been explained in the *Essays*. As James said in an effort to point out the overflow of experience:

Look where you will, you gather only examples of the same amid the different, and of different relations existing as it were in solution of the same thing. *Qua* this our experience is not the same as it is *qua* that, truly enough; but the *quas* are conceptual shots of ours at its post-mortem remains, and in its sensational immediacy everything is all at once whatever different things it is at once at all.[75]

The chapters on Fechner and Bergson paid a public debt that James felt was due; and, more important, they established the preliminaries for the concluding two lectures. As concerned the debt, James saw thinkers such as the two he discussed as constituting a growing alternative tradition; Fechner, Bergson, and their like were "wild beasts of the philosophic desert" that needed to be brought to public attention.[76] As for the quitting of preliminaries, the lectures on these two men gave James the opportunity to explain the technical details of his vision, and to orient his listeners to the kinds of depictions that could be expected. With this done, James could forgo further demonstration; he could display the heart and center of his vision.

What emerged from James's final description was a world full of mystery, a drama of religious bindings and communions none of which, any more than was the case with the mystical experiences of the *Varieties*, could be proven but whose facticity could not be denied by those who had recognized their presence.[77] It was also a world full of the presence of absence; that was the source of the mystery, after all, that a fact of failure could be overcome, that continuity was forged across gaps that could not be breached. Finally, it was a world shot through with moments of miracle, where possibility ended and power ran out, and then a "more" of power arose, and a depth of possibility, a salvation of sorts from a present impossibility.

When James described the continuity of experience, it was like a repeating period of religious ecstasy, of quite literal standing outside oneself, cutting across old borders toward a fuller frontier. What resulted was the dogging of the negative within the minimal fact, an "apparition of difference" in every experience that was the experience's end of being and the spring of its future power to be. Experience meant a confrontation of fact with fact, of something with an other, an act and event where something was bound to be.

In every crescendo of sensation, in every effort to recall, in every progress towards the satisfaction of desire, this succession of an emptiness and fullness that have reference to each other and are one flesh is the essence of the phenomenon. In every hindrance of desire the sense of an ideal presence which is absent in fact, of an absent, in a word, which the only function of the present is to *mean*, is even more notoriously there.[78]

And when, in turn, James described the fact of salvation, the continuity of experience at its most powerful and profound, it was as a kind of transdescendence, a cutting not just across but into and through unyielding limits, a full change in that the very definitions of life were being re-bound into a wider framework of power and meaning. Religious experience, at its deepest, was this experience of transformation, the advent and establishment of life where there was no life but only life's coming to a halt; it was the presence of continuing relation in the relation of absence, where there was nothing at all. When existence came up empty, indigent, and unholy, experience could be truly revolutionary, not just the experience of an obstacle being removed but of a way of life being overturned, of a death being overcome, led again into life: "Here is a world in which all is well, in spite of certain forms of death, indeed because of certain forms of death—death of hope, death of strength, death of responsibility, of fear and worry, competency and desert, death of everything that paganism, naturalism, and legalism pin their faith on and tie their trust to."[79]

With mystical experience and communion now embedded at the heart of the world's life, James brought his description to a close, again by way of warning. The world that James envisioned, that *multum in parvo*[80] of experience fully bound, converted and converting, was not the hero's world of self-assertion; it was predicated on acquiescence and consent, on the giving up of control. Neither was it the heroic world of simple good and grace, a world that was finally well founded. Communion ran with radical disunion and inalterable disjunction; bindings were as often as not incomplete; they broke down and were never re-established. Some things simply got left out, as James explained it; his vision was, again, of a twice-born, sick-souled world and not of a once-born cosmos already complete. At every turn, even with its mysteries of continuity and salvation, it remained a world with contingency at its base. There was always a chance that life was bound nowhere.

In other words, the world of James's vision was none other than the world of everyday experience, a world that matched the mundane temperament of life and held close to the understanding of the sick-souled, those "best qualified in our circle of knowledge to have experience, to tell us what is."[81] Existence was as it seemed to be to them, not already complete but just possibly able to be completed; in turn, it was a call to work in the concrete situation, and not to repose in the purity of an abstract, absolute realm. And as there were other, more than human powers at work, so too were they as they ordinarily appeared to be: not the God of the philosophers, lifting us up to a starry, unsullied realm, but rather the gods of rivers and deserts and trees, in and of the world, breaking it up along with the rest of us, active and uninterested and always bound by experience's relations. James wrote:

> I can hardly conceive of anything more different from the absolute than the God, say, of David or of Isaiah. That God is an essentially finite being in the cosmos, not with the cosmos in him . . . and if you say that the notion of the absolute is what the gods of Abraham, of David and of Jesus, after first developing into each other, were inevitably destined to develop into in more reflective modern minds, I reply that altho in certain philosophical minds this may have been the case, in minds more properly to be termed religious the development has followed quite another path.[82]

James's description was now finished. It was a "definite alternative" to the view of life in the abstract; it held out for all to see "the actual peculiarities of the world." Of course, nothing in the description could be proven fully; it was a description, after all, of "life exceeding logic," a pragma leading back into experience rather than summing it up from above. And thus it was a matter of faith, or, as James now called it, the "will to believe."[83] But as a way both of seeing and of acting after having seen, a way that took account of the facts, it was not merely a dream but a hypothesis with a chance of becoming true; it was a will to believe in which James felt there was every right to believe.

Conclusion

If only we arrange our life according
to that principle which counsels us
that we must always hold to the difficult,
then that which now still seems to us
the most alien will become what we
most trust and find most faithful.

Rainer Maria Rilke, *Letters*

"Call it 'A beginning of an introduction to philosophy,'" James said of his last, unfinished project, a textbook in "metaphysics."[1] He could have said the same thing about his work overall. For whatever else James's work may have been, it was at all points a beginning, still lacking in rigid distinctions, the kind of work in which the same thing could be seen and named differently. And even when James was most convinced, there was still an openness to his explanations, a pause for other considerations. He always came to a halt before coming to a conclusion. None of this should be taken pejoratively; indeed, just the opposite. To borrow from a remark made by Goethe: "The original thinkers are still conscious of the insoluble core of their project, and attempt to approach it in a naive and flexible manner. The successors are inclined to become didactic, and their dogmatism, gradually, reaches the level of intolerance."[2]

If the quotation from James is appropriate as a general description of his work, it is even more so as a statement about the content and meaning of that work. To be sure, part of the reason why James's explanations remained as flexible as they did was his manner of approach; the more sufficient reason, however, was that what he was explaining required such an open form and expression. To be a beginner, for James, entailed not just a frame of mind but a matter of understanding, a recognition that the center of his vision determined that he not proceed much beyond beginning. Conviction coupled with consent gave James's explanations their plasticity; both together brought him to reject dogmatism and final, uncompromising statement.

What proved to be so determinative in James's work, and what formed the center of his vision, has been variously described: a world ever not quite; a plural universe as yet unfinished, really growing, with its windows and doors wide open. At its core, however, there was that "theatre of possibilities," the play of experience as a free, contingent realm, "so that the next turn in events can at any given moment genuinely be ambiguous , i.e., possibly this, but also possibly that."[3] What bound the self was uncertainty; put slightly differently, what mattered in life were all of its "maybes" and "ifs." When James looked at experience, he saw it as a flowing stream of the old mixed with the new, a pattern of continual creation in which novelty played a significant part.

As possibility was the key to the center of the Jamesian universe, it served too as the hinge on which all of the other elements in that universe turned. The radii from that central fact, the various functions of experience as thoughts and things, people and endeavors and projects and dreams: all of these outbuildings from the experiential core were in turn determined by that core; they existed, for James, as functions and relations grounded in possibility. "Did or did not the first morning of creation write what the last dawn of reckoning shall read?"[4] James asked; and his answer was a definite no. To speak of the world as a matter of possibilities was to say that the world was open in all directions. More than that, it was to say that the world had its own integrity, was not a copy or something made up in advance.

"Possibility," James wrote in his unfinished "introduction," "as distinguished from necessity on the one hand and from impossibility on the other, is an essential category of human thinking."[5] It was also more than that for James; because possibility was one way of human thinking, it was not just a category but the adequate characterization of all conception. Thought was basically a kind of belief, an attitude or faith, a matter of hypothetical propositions. This was so not only out of deference to the ambiguous, contingent nature of things but also because thought was of the nature of things, part and parcel of the world of contingent experience. Thought as belief or faith was "one of the inalienable birthrights of our mind. Of course it must remain a practical and not a dogmatic attitude. It must go with toleration of other faiths, with the search for the most probable, and with the full consciousness of responsibilities and risks."[6]

And as thought was a matter of possibility, so also was every other kind of activity. Action was, quite simply, the flow of experience into its next, the grounding of the world of possible experience in partial realizations. In his final work James talked again about "activity situations,"[7] the fact that everything was held in a solution of other things that had not yet, and quite possibly might not, come to be. Experience in its function as activity was a creation growing, quite literally groaning, leading out from itself, seeking for itself a fulfilment in something else that, by itself, it could not be.

Finally, as possibility formed the heart of the world of experience, so it determined the understanding of the ultimate powers at work in that world. The "more" to life, the possibility of powers wider than and at work alongside those of everyday experience, could not be ruled out, and, given the facts of experience, more than likely had to be ruled in. Such was the depth of possibility in the Jamesian view, that even with the fact of final failure, of experience possibly leading nowhere, the overcoming of that failure very well could be. But as possibility opened out into wider frameworks of power, so it also bound them in: the "more" to life was always just a "more," not an all or an absolute. To talk of wider powers and of the depth of possibility in the world could not mean that possibility was annulled.

Thus, while James saw a world of experience that was fully a world of creation, it was not a creation whose center or circumference was guaranteed. To see possibility at the center of things did not mean to catch sight of the world as some innocent first-growth garden. The world was not an unspoiled tract but a land at least in part laid waste. To be poised at the leading edge of creation was to be placed not in a world that was good but in a world that was conditioned through and through by the imperative "Let it be good."⁸ And as the center of the world was no Edenic setting but a life on the border, so its end and extension was not some necessary final blessed state but only a provisional place, a utopia in the best sense of the word, construed as a historical project. Finally, it was a place that only *might* be gained, and definitely not by some inevitable process; if the good was to be let in, it would have to be by risks and wagers and repeated acts of strategic regeneration. "The world," as James put it, "may be saved, on condition that its parts shall do their best. But shipwreck in detail, or even on the whole, is among the open possibilities."⁹

"This is, so far as I know," said George Santayana about James's work, "a new philosophical vista; it is a conception never before presented, although implied, perhaps, in various quarters."¹⁰ Taking into account a degree of overstatement in Santayana's claim as well as a conscious ignoring of other streams of thought that were moving along with James's way of thinking, one may agree with his statement. James had defined the two dominant poles of thinking in his day and had used both to run a third course in between them: on the one hand, he had become more radically empiricist than the materialists and positivists, and had turned their vision of a dead, mechanical world into one of vitality and conjunctive relations; and on the other, he had become more romantic than the idealists and high romanticists, had taken their flight above the world and redirected it, plunging it back down into everyday facts until they became ideal leadings and real adventures. "There shall be news," James was fond of saying, quoting from a poem by a friend; "there shall be news in Heaven."¹¹ And there was news on earth as well. Indeed, what James offered was not just a new philosophical vision but a vision of the new, essentially a new world vision.

There was, of course, a price to be paid for all the news that James gave in his descriptions; the new world of experience had different assumptions behind it and raised different hopes than were customary. James restored a sense of power to the human scene, something close to a Nietzschean notion of gaiety. It was a power, however, that was properly only a power of relation; it could become a pure will to power only by distorting what power was meant to be. And he provided a sense of productive purpose to work and endeavor, although it was not a purpose that was immutable and eternal but, finally, gratuitous, for nothing and for free. When all was said and done, "The phantom of an attitude, the echo of a certain mode of thought, a few pages of print, some invention, or some victory gained in a brief critical hour, are all that can survive the best of us."[12]

Where the price was paid most dearly, perhaps, was in the news that James brought about the religious life. Gone was the world of monotheistic security, and in its place was an uncertain, almost animistic world of powers none of which were any more than co-creative with us. And as the God of monotheism was lost, so was that God's providential, guiding hand. There was still a creation, but it was unpremeditated; a god might still provide, but the provision would be like all other provisions, seeing its way into history rather than wrapping it up. Above all, what was lost in James's vision was religion as a reasonable endeavor. James did not explain away the crude superstitions and wildness of popular religious life and practice; rather, he built on them, used them as the defining data for his explanations. All of which made for a priesthood of all believers, and for an openness to incursions of all sorts, that was unsettling.

But James gave as he took away, and what he gave may have been more than worth the loss. What he provided in his vision was a religious world—indeed, a religious world three times over. First, James offered a picture of the universe as religiously based, a description of the world in which the facts were not dead but alive and at work, were pragma not only capable of being but indeed bound to be something more than mere matters of fact. Stated slightly differently, as experience was reducible to the experience of possibility, so possibility was but another name for the presence of an apparition of difference, the existence of a problem and its solution—in a word, James's definition of religion as he had stated it in the *Varieties*.[13] Religion was not a name just for an aspect of experience but for experience's fundamental dimension. The "more" to be gained from religion was not of some world apart, or of some special part of the world, but rather of the very structure and way of the world overall.

Second, as the world was religious in a general way, so also it was religious in a definite sense, when construed as existence and a life lived in the world. James took the notion of faith seeking understanding and turned it to fit his model of experience: existence meant to be placed on a "faith ladder," moving from rung to rung by acts of belief.[14] To live was to live forward, constantly seeking and outstripping the status quo; it was to be bound to a "more" as desire is bound to its object, unsatisfied until that object is attained. What was being sought, however, was not a rational understanding but a practical way of life, the verification of beliefs in relations of fulfillment. By the end of his work, James had expanded his will to believe until it had become the description of all human life, and not simply of life at its moments of crisis. Or rather, James had come to define the character of all life as a matter of crisis, existence on the edge of the old and the new, restless but in a positive way, as an expression of and consent to the fact of possibility.

In his *Principles of Psychology* James gave a description of this definite religious quality of life, one he did not allow full play in his early work but which summarizes well his overall point of view. Life was not simply a matter of faith but more properly a matter of prayer; it was that peculiar way of being by submitting, living under the impact of a question, longing rather than mere idle curiosity. More specifically, it was a questioning for quite definite purposes, concrete possibilities, and specific ends:

> We hear, in these days of scientific enlightment, a great deal of discussion about the efficacy of prayer; and many reasons are given us why we should not pray, whilst others are given us why we should. But in all of this very little is said of the reason why we *do* pray, which is simply that we cannot help praying. It seems probable that, in spite of all that "science" may do to the contrary, man will continue to pray to the end of time.[15]

The world as religious overall, that is, as the possibility of experience, and life in the world as a constant, prayerful, seeking: these two received their third and final complement in an understanding of specific religious moments, when the self and society confronted the limits of possibility and stood asking for something more, and there appeared a wider power able to bring something new—an impossible possibility—from that which was all for naught. In this third sense of the religious nature of things, James looked at experience not merely as a movement of life that outstripped the present evidence but as a projection, quite literally a way of being thrown over existence's gaps. Here experience was found to be radically creative, a matter of leaps and cuts across the historical limits of life. Again, however, these moments of transcendence were within the experiential flow: the experience of divinity was an experience that fulfilled the everyday need for a "more" to life but did not overstep it or cancel it out. The specific way of religious life was not an exception, according to James, as much as it was an extreme case of the relations that obtained in mundane life, where everything was stretched to the point where it showed its true meaning and nature, where the structure of what possibility actually meant was most clearly revealed.[16]

All that James gave in his vision of religion and life can be brought down to this: he provided a way of seeing the religious world and the practical, everyday world as one. In the terms of the debate going on in his day, James collapsed the distinctions between religion, science, and morality. These became three ways of taking the same fact: belief *was* inquiry and practice and was not apart from them.[17] James, that is, offered a definition of religion as a way of life, as the description of one's total orientation. Religion was not a static abstraction or system of doctrines but an active engagement, a way of being committed, how we are bound at any point to be. Nor was activity apart from its being as belief; unless one sought to restrict religion to its narrowest definition and meaning, then all activity had a religious quality, had to do with that "dumb sense of what life honestly and deeply means."[18]

As there was a general price to be paid for accepting the world on James's terms, there was also a specific cost in one's status as a person. Here we may begin to return to the social context in which James worked. That is, there was a particular cost for those who held to mainstream, middle-class definitions of persons as distinct, separative individuals. Gone now from James's redescription were almost all the individualistic habits and securities, accepted patterns of behavior and aspiration. The privileged position that looked on life from above had been relinquished for the sake of a relative view from below. To lie in the middle of experience meant that the observational gaze had to be given up. Along with that, of course, went the security of the once-born life: the guarantees of absolute claims made before the fact; the comforts of not having to deal with relations; the luxury of being able to lead one's life under the dimension of control. Finally, there was the loss of the sense that life could ever be overcome. The route to higher truth was cut off; the dream of a life in correspondence with the truth was shattered against the necessity of having to undergo the conditions of experience.[19]

This personal cost of accepting James's view, what amounted to a certain pain of growth denied, had as its counterpart a greater growing pain, what James had called the "inner catastrophe," which arose from the adoption of his outlook and vision. First, there was the pain entailed in ceasing to live one's own story and in giving up control. There was also the pain of the turn to experience; for what was required here was an act of disappropriation, a submission of the will, a breaking through of all the limits that had kept the person individually bound. Last of all, there was a lifelong pain to be felt as one began to live from this new perspective: the pain of being overwhelmed by the wealth of life's relations and the recognition that none of who and what one was came with any guarantee. The greatest comfort that could be given was this, as James put it, quoting from an ancient Greek epitaph: "A ship-wrecked sailor, buried on this coast, bids thee take sail. Full many a gallant ship, when we were lost, weathered the gale."[20]

All of this may seem overly dramatic, but it is not. In asking for his view to be granted authority, James demanded a change of the springs underlying people's actions and thoughts; he called for a radical conversion, a total redirection of vision, death to an old, outmoded self and rebirth into a new way of life. The path to overcoming led through a crisis that had to be undergone; unless one wished to be merely an advocate, seeing the old and naming it as such but not moving away, recognizing the new and calling for it to be brought about but without turning to it, then some kind of painful, even tragic passage from the old world to the new had to be undertaken.

As the general price of accepting James's vision was in part religious, so too was there a religious cost being exacted and a religious crisis to be endured. What stood to be lost was the traditional route of salvation, the well-lit path of steady, predictable progress away from the flux of uncertainty, beyond the reach of conflict and struggle and possible defeat. James's vision reversed the route, perhaps even cut it off; to accept what James offered meant that salvation would be found, if at all, only under the conditions of immanent, historical life. All of which brought on the crisis, for history was always "ever not quite," never more than penultimately, possibly secure. And that meant that the religious life, the life of seeking salvation, would be a series of conversions, a constant canceling out of one penultimate by the next, only possibly more ultimate fact. With every conversion there would be a moment of forsaking, where one would have to turn away from that whose measure of good was not good enough; then seeking would have that edge of despair that is the other side of hope, and the seeker would know the thinness of the border between the religious and the insane.

Once more, however, the benefits of taking up James's way of seeing may have outweighed the costs that were exacted, and the crisis may have been worth undergoing. To begin with, James had restored a sense of vitality and a measure of cooperative meaning to the religious and saintly life. Religion was now a program of work; it was not a path of detachment and privacy but a route of radical and public commitment. And as the religious life was at all points a movement within the facts of experience, a matter of immanent possibilities, so it allowed for a continual re-evaluation of one's concrete options, indeed, demanded that present, unsatisfactory, and penultimate situations be converted and overcome. "Not unfortunately," James wrote, quoting from Benjamin Blood, "the universe is wild, game-flavored as a hawk's wing. Nature is miracle all. She knows no laws; the same returns not, save to bring the different."[21]

And as the universe was genuinely open, a continual creation and conversion and change, so the religious life need not, indeed could not, be doctrinaire and dogmatic but had to be flexible, subject in its vision to critique and reform. Faith now meant responsibility—an ability to respond—analysis and imagination combined. It gave warrant and support to the human capacity to discern the spirits in a given situation, to project the unseen from the seen, to trace the implications of events into a next event that was still not yet, and to stake a claim that here, even if only for now, could be found the images and shadows of divine things. To be sure, this avowal of the imaginative capacity could lead to all sorts of projections, which analysis might not be able to contain. But better this risk of an illusory faith, James argued, than the risk of a faith where nothing could be ventured and everything remained always the same.[22]

Finally, as James's vision opened religion to the facts of experience, so in turn it opened experience to the facts of religion. The religious life was no longer a life in a world apart. It carried into all aspects of work and endeavor, was inclusive of every kind of project in which people placed their hopes. At the same time, it could not be excluded from any arena of activity; it had a claim wherever statements of belief were made, wherever people were engaged in action and reflection. There was a partial exception, for in the encounters with the wider powers of divinity, one did become engaged in a genuinely unusual event. Even here, however, the encounter had to do with the immanent world of everyday experience. It was an experience that moved one not out of history but from one historical situation into another.

Americans walked away from James's work with great praise and greater speed. They did so in the years immediately following his death and have continued to do so to this day. The self and world that James described received, and have continued to receive, much comment but little testing as serious alternatives. The news that he announced as coming to the fore has been for the most part either ignored or chastened to the point where it could seem like an announcement of something else. In the decades since his death, mainstream, middle-class American culture has continued with scarcely a halt along its high-romantic path.[23] Shapers of the culture have seen little value in a world with no metaphysical comfort; they have continued to be captivated by a vision of a world clinched in an all-encompassing embrace. Put somewhat differently, the predominant cultural outlook has continued to be imperialistic, a vision of the world in which the only possibility that exists is the possibility of One. Few have taken heed of the plural, relational universe to which James pointed, and when they have, all too often they have construed it against the grain of James's thought, taken it as a matter not of some but of all or none.

Fewer still have seen any value in James's religious formulations and explanations, his piecemeal supernaturalism and panpsychism, his twice-born and saintly self. Here, perhaps more than anywhere else, James's work has consistently been corrected in quite definite directions: where his religious explanations have not been rejected, they have been revised upward, adjusted so that his description of a contingent world seeking salvation has become some first sight of a predestined shore, a land of monotheistic security and total reconciliation of parts with the whole. Once again, James's work has been re-placed into the high-romantic tradition that he struggled to overcome. Where James depicted religion as a ship of faith, bound for an uncertain and uncharted end, now the description has been undone, turned into a picture of a ship of fate headed straight forward with scarcely a wave, let alone a storm, to challenge its course. And where James saw those who were religious as being in essence a crew composed of castaways and renegades, they have been recast into a gathering of uniformed, respectable, and above all organized sailors at all times working efficiently and in unison. As was the case with James's description overall, his religious outlook has been taken over rather than carried out. It has been ordered, indeed incorporated, in every sense of the word.[24]

This should not be taken to mean that James has been forgotten by the custodians of American culture; in fact he has become something of an idol of popular fancy. But this has had the effect of subverting his efforts. The praise has gone to James the man and not to his work. James has become a hero of sorts, a genius and inspirer, an example of an exceptional individual and a member of an extraordinary family.[25] And when his work has been evaluated, it has been seen as a system, not the "grammar of action"[26] that he tried to show it to be, but rather a total philosophy with its logic, its whither and its whence, all within the confines of the internal logic of ideas. Then, of course, James's work becomes without responsibility, save, perhaps, to other systems of thought. The reversal of values that he tried to bring to light, the understanding of philosophy as a reflection on human practice, is averted away from the stream of life, toward a stream of disengaged, abstract thought.

Neither is this intended to imply that James has been without a professional following: scholars of all sorts have continued to pay their respects to what he had to say, and to borrow from his understandings. Here again, however, the borrowing has often seemed a misuse and manipulation. Where James tried to weave together various ways of thinking in his description, now those ways have once again been taken apart. Thus, for example, scholars with a positivistic outlook and agenda ha۷ ۵ taken James's "tough-mindedness" and empiricism as support for their claims and have used the holistic side of his work as a corrective to their more atomistic doctrines. They have done this, however, while ignoring his stress on contingency and his criticisms of objectivism, scientism, and correspondence theories of truth.[27] Idealists, in turn, have claimed his voice of social hope and his assertion of the integrity of belief. They have used James, this time minus much of his empiricism (and his nonfoundationalism), to support their quests for deep "cosmic purposes" and for "the nature of the highest reality."[28] Others have taken fragments and pieces of James's work: psychologists have held on to his understanding of "attention"; ethicists and social critics have made use of his rhetoric about the "moral equivalent of war"; theologians and philosophers of religion have explored the implications of the "will to believe" and religious experience. In short, James's work has been treated as if it were a storehouse of formulas and slogans suitable for any cultural project whatsoever. Few have seen fit to take up his understandings with any regard for his own cultural project.

Finally, none of this is meant to ignore the pragmatist tradition in which, to at least some extent, James thought his work would be carried out. That tradition did continue after James's death; indeed, it has continued, at least until the 1950s, with a measure of cultural success, at various points verging on breaking through the dominant cultural mainstream of high romance.[29] Here, at least at first glance, the integrity of James's description appears to have received the respect it was due. His understanding of the contingency of human starting points has been upheld, and stemming from that, his recognition that human quests for certainty are at best nonproductive. James's core of convictions has been kept intact: that our tasks are not heroic but are more a matter of muddling through; that our lives are not absolute but epic affairs, at best something that can be made to hang together; finally, that the criterion by which we should evaluate our lives is not knowledge or truth or the right but the concrete, mundane difference that is made by what we do.[30]

As pragmatists have tended to respect James's central convictions, they have also heeded his call for an antiessentialist, practicalist, and immanentist cultural orientation and reflection. Cultural projects have been undertaken that attempt to get people through and past their "metaphysical need." Communities have begun to be envisioned in which this-worldly solidarity (instead of transcendent unity) is "the only comfort," and is seen to be "good enough." Finally, thoroughgoing redescriptions have been carried out that are predicated upon James's fundamental philosophical characterizations of "knowledge as nonfoundational inquiry, reason as nontranscendent or immanent criticism, every sort of language as expressive, imaginative, or poetic, every part of existence as contingent and historical, and philosophy itself as a reflection on problems of human finitude rather than a search for first principles or for the really real."[31]

All of this respect for and continuance of James's work by later pragmatists represents agreement, and it is tempting to see it as thorough. But just as pragmatists have tended to stand with James on his antiessentialism, they have also tended to strip away from his redescription the richness of his religious understandings. What James called his "religious or quasi-religious philosophy" has become at times a mild humanism with a general appeal to a "common faith," and at its most severe an antireligious, aggressively secularist project aimed at seeing what difference it would make to live according to the norm that nothing is to be worshipped. And where James valorized the saint and the self of conversion and submission, later pragmatists have valorized the scientist and, more recently, the strong poet, figures who refuse to submit to anything "out there."[32]

Perhaps the best way to explain this shift from James to the later pragmatists is to say that where James called for a de-absolutized cultural formation, those who came after him have called for a de-divinized formation. James saw pragmatism as affording, at the level of religious bindings, a way to appreciate the complexity of things, the fact that, as he put it, "the plot of possibilities thickens."[33] Pragmatism for James was a project of re-engagement, an attempt to replace the self back into its environing field. In turn, James saw pragmatism as an opportunity to break through his culture's monistic fascination, the spell cast by the word *one*. Pragmatism did away with monism in all of its forms: in its religious form of monotheism, the worship of the One God, One truth, and One right way; in its social form of the once-born life, in which all was in the single, separative self's control; in its philosophical form, in which otherness, relationality and co-creativity were defects that had to be taken up and made into one; finally, in its political and bureaucratic form in which everything was reduced to the rule of one, and in which everything had to be done one way.

Later pragmatists, by contrast, have looked to pragmatism with different ends in view. Simply put, they have seen pragmatism as a way to continue and complete the Enlightenment project of human prediction and control; as Kant defined it, "the outgoing of human-kind from self-inflicted dependencies." Pragmatism here has been taken as affording an opportunity to keep understandings of power within humanistic bounds. With its emphasis on contingency, it can provide a way to bracket out notions of supernatural powers and gods; with its emphasis on the unavailability of any "real" world out there waiting to be found, it can give a sense of human creative making as the only making around. Thus, where the goal of prag-matism was for James a life re-engaged with all sorts of possibili-ties, the goal has become a life that is independent, separated from all but the possibility of becoming a self-made person. Pragmatism, it now is hoped, is a cultural project that will "culminate in our no longer being able to see any use for the notion that finite, mortal, contingently existing human beings might derive the meanings of their lives from anything except other finite, mortal, contingently existing human beings."[34]

What all of this tracing of James's work in its aftermath is intended to say is that the legacy of James's work has been at its best a narrowed pragmatic redescription cut loose from its context in a world of possibilities (only some of which are human), plurali-ties, and religious bindings. James's understanding of pragma as the liveliness of experience—"live options," a world filled with all sorts of vital forces—has been drained of all its life: right action has ceased to be right relations with and respect for all that is at work in the world and has fallen to the level of expediencies, consequences, and warranted assertions; right belief has become simply a matter of deciding what works and not, as James had it, also an evaluation and discovery of what is already in the making. In turn, James's pluralistic universe has been returned to a monistic, albeit human-centered base. The world is dead and mechanical again, a literal realm of brute fact; the prevailing notion has become that pragmatism has "no room for the notion that there are nonhuman forces to which human beings should be responsible."[35] Last, and as a result of the two preceding turns, James's world of experience has been denied: as creativity has been limited to human making, so the notion that one can find oneself bound this way or that has been ruled out. As there are again only human forces at work, so a twice-born life of consent, submission, and conversion makes no sense, needs to be recast into a life of assertion and control.

Now, some will say that all of this movement away from James has been for the best, that the most of James's work that can be abided at present is the nonfoundational humanism of his pragmatic revisionists; that the pluralism, panpsychism, and religious world that James projected would simply lead us back into the kinds of religious fanaticisms, wills to power, and wills to truth that historically have done so much harm. Others will claim that it is better, at least for now, that America keep to the completion of its Enlightenment project: perhaps, until we have a stronger understanding of our own creative possibilities, we would be better off leaving out James's call to a life of submission; perhaps in this day and age the carrying out of any project of a twice-born, humble life would lead only to humiliation.

It has been both the purpose and the argument of this book to say that these claims need not be correct, indeed that the revisioning of James's work since his death has been something of a shame. While I do not claim that those who came after James have been wrong in their revisionist proposals and projections—that, after all, would be to say, against James's recognition about contingency, that James got something right—they may have missed a chance that would have been worth the effort to pursue. Indeed, the chance that they may have missed seems to be the chance to overcome the very problems that were feared would result should James's project genuinely be taken up. Simply put, the shame in giving up on all that James was about in his work may be that it has left us still caught in cultural formations that breed fanaticism and humiliation.

Stated somewhat more positively, the chance that James's work envisioned, and that it has been the task of this book to bring back to mind, is the chance to break through what may be the real culprits in our current American cultural projects: not religion but the monotheistic construction of religion; not self-submission but the monarchical construction of the self as a separate individual for whom the only satisfying, nonhumiliating life is a life in which "thus I willed it" is the goal.[36] James projected that giving one's life up and over, undergoing experience rather than trying to overcome it, would lead to a way of life that was gratifying. To submit oneself into life was for James a fitting way to be in a world come of age. At the same time, he wagered that treating all of life as if it mattered as much as oneself, being open and receptive and cooperative, striving not to recreate so much as to be co-creative, would lead us beyond a life whose watchword was control. To admit that one's way was among and along with many, more than that, to consent to being one and many, was, for James, an appropriate style of life in a world where we are trying not to be right but to be free.

NOTES

William James will be cited as WJ throughout the notes.

Introduction

1. For examples of these two tendencies in James scholarship, see Richard Rorty's treatment of James in *Consequences of Pragmatism* (Minneapolis: University of Minnesota Press, 1982), and Wayne Proudfoot's treatment of James in *Religious Experience* (Berkeley: University of California Press, 1985). Rorty dislocates James's self-redescriptions from his religious understandings, and as a result makes James into a nonfoundationalist and romantic strong poet. Proudfoot dislocates James's religious investigations from the rest of his work, and as a result comes up with a James who is basically a Schleiermachian or naive romantic, one who talks about religious experience without any awareness of the contingency and contextualization of that experience.

2. Lewis Mumford, *Technics and Human Development* (New York: Harcourt Brace Jovanovich, 1967), p. 16.

3. The specific allusion here is to Jacques Barzun, *A Stroll with William James* (New York: Harper and Row, 1983), where James is treated as a contemporary conversation partner. Henry Levinson, in *The Religious Investigations of William James* (Chapel Hill: University of North Carolina Press, 1981), raises the problem of "presentism" in James scholarship. While his point may be somewhat overstated, I agree with Levinson that James must be considered with regard for his time and place.

4. For an assessment of James's understanding of his responsibility to society, see Nicholas Lash, *Easter in Ordinary* (Charlottesville: University of Virginia Press, 1988), pp. 21–23.

5. For a strictly biographical work on James, see Gay Wilson Allen, *William James: A Biography* (New York: Viking, 1967). Ralph Barton Perry's two-volume *Thought and Character of William James* (Boston: Little, Brown, 1935) offers the most exhaustive treatment of James's per-

sonal and intellectual context; see also the more recent treatment by Gerald Meyers, *William James: His Life and Thought* (New Haven: Yale University Press, 1986). Finally, for a text treating James's letters and relationships and their basis for his work, see Daniel Bjork, *William James: The Center of His Vision* (New York: Columbia University Press, 1988).

6. The phrase, although widely used, is borrowed from Paul Carter; see his *Spiritual Crisis of the Gilded Age* (DeKalb: Northern Illinois University Press, 1971).

7. Jeffrey Stout, *Ethics After Babel* (Boston: Beacon Press, 1988), esp. chap. 10.

8. Lash, *Easter in Ordinary*, p. 24.

9. There were, it should be said here, other "selves" at work in James's early writings, alternatives to the image that he drew in the *Principles* (and in turn images upon which he would draw as he began to move away from his self-description in the psychology). For an example of such an alternative self, see James's introductory essay in *The Literary Remains of Henry James*, ed. William James (Boston: James R. Osgood and Co., 1885).

10. It should be noted here that James did not simply turn away from his earlier work. As I argue in chapters 4 and 5, he returned to the *Principles*, and to other early works, and drew from them understandings that, in the *Principles*, had remained for the most part marginal and only partially filled out. James's later works are best understood, I believe, as a re-vision, a seeing again, of thoughts that were present but were not fully realized.

11. Rorty, *Consequences of Pragmatism*, p. xlii. For a discussion of these two tendencies in twentieth-century American thought, see the whole of Rorty's introduction in *Consequences*.

12. Stout, *Ethics After Babel*, p. 191. It should be noted here that Stout is in conversation with Alasdair MacIntyre and is making, in part, MacIntyre's point.

13. Simone de Beauvoir, *The Second Sex*, trans. H. M. Parshley (New York: Vintage Books, 1974), p. xxxiii.

14. Carol Christ, "Rethinking Theology and Nature," in *Weaving the Visions*, ed. Judith Plaskow and Carol Christ (San Francisco: Harper Collins, 1989), p. 321. Those with whom I find my work to be most in league are, among the "pragmatists," Henry Levinson and Jeffrey Stout (see Stout's, *Ethics After Babel* and Levinson's "Pragmatic Naturalism and the Spiritual Life," *Raritan* 10 [Fall 1990]: 70–86), and, among the feminists, particularly Katherine Keller (see her *From a Broken Web* [Boston: Beacon Press]).

15. Stout, *Ethics After Babel*, p. 170.

Chapter 1

1. The term *neurasthenia* was coined by George Miller Beard in *American Nervousness: Its Causes and Consequences* (New York: G. P. Putnam's Sons, 1881); it was a general descriptive term covering any number of disorders stemming from what Beard called a lack of nerve force given the exigencies of civilization. See his chapter "Causes of American Nervousness," and also the study by Tom Lutz, *American Nervousness, 1903* (Ithaca: Cornell University Press, 1991).

2. *The Letters of William James*, ed. Henry James (Boston: Atlantic Monthly Press, 1920), 1:158. The letter was written during James's period of invalidism and neurasthenic crisis, which lasted roughly from 1869 to 1871.

3. Henry Ward Beecher, "The Advance of a Century," *New York Tribune*, extra 33 (July 4, 1876), reprinted in Alan Trachtenberg, *Democratic Vistas* (New York: George Braziller, 1970), p. 70.

4. Beecher, "The Advance of a Century," p. 70.

5. The passage is from *Henry IV*, and was quoted by William James in his address "Is Life Worth Living?" in *The Will to Believe and Other Essays in Popular Philosophy* (New York: Longmans, Green, 1897), p. 62.

6. Lewis Mumford, *Brown Decades* (New York: Harcourt, Brace, 1931), p. 6.

7. See Walt Whitman, "Democracy," *Galaxy* 4 (1867): 933.

8. Quoted from Adolphe De Chambrun, *Impressions of Lincoln and the Civil War: A Foreigner's Account* (New York: Random House, 1952), p. 83. For an analysis of Lincoln's attitude toward the war, see George Forgie, *Patricide in the House Divided* (New York: W. W. Norton, 1979), chap. 7, "Abraham Lincoln and the Melodrama of the House Divided."

9. Elizabeth Stuart Phelps, *The Gates Ajar* (Boston: Fields, Osgood, 1869), p. 73. Phelps's novel was one of a number of eschatological novels to be published in the decade after the Civil War.

10. The *Discourses* were reworked and published in 1861 under the title *Christian Nurture* (New York: Charles Scribner, 1861). For a discussion of the culture of domesticity, see Ann Douglas, *The Feminization of American Culture* (New York: Avon Books, 1977).

11. Sociological analysis supporting these claims can be found in Stephan Thernstrom, *The Other Bostonians* (Cambridge, MA: Harvard University Press, 1973); see esp. chap. 2, "Population Growth, Migration, and Turnover."

12. E. L. Godkin, "Chromo-Civilization," *Nation* 19 (1874): 202. Godkin goes on to write that "a society of ignoramuses each of which thinks he

is a Solon, would be an approach to Bedlam let loose, and something analogous to this may really be seen today." The subject of the editorial was the Beecher-Tilton scandal.

13. In *The Works of James Russell Lowell* (Boston: Houghton Mifflin, 1890), 10:96.

14. S. M. Campbell, "Christianity and Civil Liberty," *American Presbyterian and Theological Review* 5 (1867): 390–91. For an analysis of the religious responses to the changing social definitions in the decade following the Civil War, see Henry May, *Protestant Churches and Industrial America* (New York: Harper and Brothers, 1949), chap. 11. More will be said later on about the religious responses.

15. Walt Whitman, "Going Somewhere," in *The Complete Writings of Walt Whitman* (New York: G. P. Putnam's Sons, 1902), p. 311. The poem originally appeared in *November Boughs* (Philadelphia: David McKay, 1888).

16. Walt Whitman, "The Dismasted Ship," in *Complete Writings*, p. 320. Again, the original publication was in *November Boughs*.

17. On the rise of "scientific management" techniques, see Henry May, *The End of American Innocence* (New York: Alfred A. Knopf, 1959), p. 2, sec. 1. Alan Trachtenberg provides an analysis of the impact of technological developments on cultural pictures of reality in *Incorporation of America* (New York: Hill and Wang, 1982), chap. 2, "Mechanization Takes Command."

18. Ralph Waldo Emerson, "Civilization," in *Society and Solitude* (Boston: Osgood, Fields, 1870), p. 27); Oliver Wendell Holmes, "Mechanism in Thought and Morals," in *Holmes' Writings* (Cambridge, MA: Riverside Press, 1891), 8:261.

19. Harriet Beecher Stowe, "House and Home Papers," in *Writings of Harriet Beecher Stowe: Household Papers and Stories* (Boston: Houghton Mifflin, 1896), pp. 100–101.

20. Thomas A. Edison, "The Phonograph and Its Future," *North American Review* 126 (1878): 530.

21. Elizabeth Stuart Phelps, "The Tenth of January," *Atlantic Monthly* 21 (1868), reprinted in Trachtenberg, *Democratic Vistas*, p. 262.

22. James Richardson, "Travelling by Telegraph," *Scribner's Monthly* 4 (1872): 6.

23. Phillips Brooks, "The Light of the World," in *Selected Sermons*, ed. William Scarlett (New York: E. P. Dutton, 1950), p. 283.

24. James F. Findlay, *Dwight L. Moody, American Evangelist* (Chicago: University of Chicago Press, 1969), p. 307.

25. For an account of the relationship between Protestant institutional patterns and the rise of a corporate order, see Gregory Singleton, "Protes-

tant Voluntary Organizations and the Shaping of Victorian America," in
Victorian America (Philadelphia: University of Pennsylvania Press, 1976),
pp. 47–28. Standard assessments of denominational development can be
found in Sydney Mead, *The Lively Experiment* (New York: Harper and
Row, 1963), chap. 8, and Paul Carter, *The Spiritual Crisis of the Gilded
Age* (DeKalb: Norther Illinois University Press, 1971), chap. 1.

26. Henry Drummond, *The City Without a Church* (New York: James
Pott, 1893), p. 41.

27. Both of the quotations can be found in Carter, *The Spiritual Crisis*,
pp. 12, 217–18.

28. James DeKoven, "The Church of the Living God," in *Sermons
Preached on Various Occasions* (New York: D. Appleton, 1880), p. 43.

29. Charles A. Briggs, "The Alienation of Church and People," *Forum*
16 (1893): 377.

30. Quoted in R. W. B. Lewis, *American Adam* (Chicago: University of
Chicago Press, 1969), p. 39.

31. Quoted from A. V. G. Allen, *Life and Letters of Phillips Brooks*
(New York: E. P. Dutton, 1900), 3:279.

32. The quotation is from Holmes, *The Guardian Angel*, cited in Lewis,
American Adam, p. 39.

33. For a discussion of the conservative reaction to liberalism and the
emerging social gospel movement, see May, *Protestant Churches and
Industrial America*, p. 4, pp. 163–69.

34. Jonathan Baxter Harrison, "Certain Dangerous Tendencies in
American Life" (1880); reprinted in Trachtenberg, *Democratic Vistas*,
p. 182.

35. Elizabeth Cady Stanton, "Has Christianity Benefitted Woman?,"
North American Review 140 (1885): 389–90.

36. John Girdner, "Theology and Insanity," *North American Review*
168 (1899): 77. On the relationship between theology and mental health, see
also Beard, "Causes of American Nervousness"; also Addington Bruce,
"Insanity and the Nation," *North American Review* 187 (1908): 71–79.

37. For an examination of the relationship between Protestantism and
nineteenth-century understandings of Christian social responsibility, see
Herbert Gutman, "Protestantism and the American Labor Movement,"
American Historical Review 72 (1966–67): 74–101.

38. See, for example, Bushnell's concern for the "out-populating power"
of family patterns of devotion and nurture, which was intended to undercut
what he saw as the private and destructive qualities of individualistic and
revivalistic religiosity, in *Christian Nature*, chap. 8.

39. See Alisdair MacIntyre, "The Debate About God: Victorian Relevance and Contemporary Irrevelance," in *The Religious Significance of*

Atheism (New York: Columbia University Press, 1977), chap. 1, "Coming to Terms with Natural Science."

40. J. Baldwin Brown, "The Roots of the Present Unbelief," *Christian Union* 24 (1881): 268. George Miller Beard saw the revivalistic and communal groups of his day as "precious curiosities, relics or antiques that the fourteenth-century has, as it were, dropped right into the middle of the nineteenth" (*American Nervousness*, p. 4).

41. See Arthur M. Schlesinger, "A Critical Period in American Religion," in *Religion in American History*, ed. John Mulder and John Wilson (Englewood Cliffs, NJ: Prentice-Hall, 1978).

42. Phelps, *The Gates Ajar*, p. 89.

43. May, *Protestant Churches and Industrial America*, chap. 5; also May's *End of American Innocence*, chap. 3, "Scoffers."

44. Brown, "The Roots of the Present Unbelief," p. 268.

45. Borden Bowne, *Theism* (New York: American Book Co., 1887), p. 316.

46. Goldwin Smith, "The Religious Situation," *North American Review* 187 (1908): 525.

47. Herman Melville, *Pierre* (1852); quoted in F. O. Matthiessen, *American Renaissance* (New York: Oxford University Press, 1941), p. 654.

Chapter 2

1. For a review of James's academic and professional training, see the relevant chapters in Ralph Barton Perry, *The Thought and Character of William James*, 2 vols. (Boston: Little, Brown, 1935); see also Gay Wilson Allen, *William James* (New York: Viking Press, 1967).

2. The focus of this chapter will be on the two-volume *Principles of Psychology* (New York: Henry Holt, 1890). It should be noted that James also published an abridged version, *Psychology—Briefer Course* (New York: Henry Holt, 1892).

3. WJ, *Briefer Course*, p. 468. For an analysis of James's understanding of the psychologist's fallacy, see John Wild, *The Radical Empiricism of William James* (Garden City, NY: Doubleday, 1969), pp. 36–42. See also Jacques Barzun, *A Stroll with William James* (New York: Harper and Row, 1983), pp. 38–39.

4. WJ, "On a Certain Blindness in Human Beings," in *Talks to Teachers on Psychology, and to Students on Some of Life's Ideals* (New York: Henry Holt, 1899), p. 231.

5. Charles Sanders Peirce, review of the *Principles, Nation* 53 (1891): 15.

6. George Trumbull Ladd, "Psychology as So-Called Natural Science," *Philosophical Review* 1 (1891): 24–53. For James's reply to Ladd's review, see "A Plea for Psychology as a Natural Science," in *Collected Essays and Reviews*, ed. R. B. Perry (New York: Longmans, Green, 1920), pp. 316–27. Other reviews critical of James's method and perspective are J. M. Baldwin, *Science* 16 (1890): 207–8; Stanley Hall, *American Journal of Psychology* 3 (1891): 585–91. Daniel Bjork, *The Compromised Scientist* (New York: Columbia University Press, 1983), provides a general review of James's relationship with the leading schools of psychology in the United States.

7. Quoted in Elizabeth Flower and Murray Murphey, *A History of Philosophy in America*, vol. 2 (New York: G. P. Putnam's Sons, 1977, p. 642. See also the review by J. G. Schurman in *Philosophical Review* 1 (1891): 313–15.

8. William Dean Howells, "Editor's Study," *Harper's Magazine* 33 (1891): 314.

9. George Santayana, "James's Psychology," *Atlantic Monthly* 67 (1891): 553.

10. In my analysis the *Principles* is divided as follows: part one, in which James disposes of certain preliminary matters, covers chaps. 1 through 7; part two, which contains the pivotal work on the stream of consciousness and self-consciousness, comprises chaps. 8 through 16; and part three, which takes up the entire second volume (chaps. 17–28), presents James's image of the self in terms of a reflex arc. There are, of course, other ways of dividing the text; the most usual six-part division is outlined in Flower and Murphey, *History of Philosophy in America*, 2:640–41.

11. WJ, *Principles* 1:451.

12. WJ, *Principles* 1:335. The discussion here is about the sense of personal identity; as I will show, James refused to think of the self as more than a unification that comes and goes, develops and changes, with the self's states of mind. "We hear from our parents various anecdotes about our infant years. . . . That child is a foreign creature with which our present self is no more identified in feeling than it is with some stranger's living child today" (*Principles* 1:335).

13. Too little attention has been paid to James's natural-science perspective or to his effort to hold to common sense. The phenomenologists have come closest to the understanding put forth here; see, for example, part one of Wild's *Radical Empiricism*. The use of common sense here is in its most general meaning; for a discussion of the background links between James and Scottish common sense philosophy, see Bruce Kuklick, "Currents of Thought in Nineteenth Century Cambridge," in *The Rise of American*

Philosophy (New Haven: Yale University Press, 1977), pp. 5–27; Jay Wharton Fay, *American Psychology Before William James* (New Brunswick, NJ: Rutgers University Press, 1939), pt. 3, "The Period of British and German Influence."

14. WJ, *Principles* 1:278. As Jacques Barzun put it: "James grasped the nettle; that is, he made consciousness-as-we-feel-it the starting point instead of the end product; he derived the elements from the activity instead of the activity from the elements" (*Stroll with William James*, p. 48).

15. WJ, *Principles* 1:367.

16. WJ, *Briefer Course*, p. 6. See also a letter by James to Thomas Ward (1869); "I feel that we are Nature through and through, that we are wholly conditioned, that not a wiggle of our will happens save as the result of physical laws; and yet, notwithstanding, we are *en rapport* with reason. How to conceive it? Who knows?" *The Letters of William James*, ed. Henry James (Boston: Atlantic Monthly Press, 1920), 1:152–53.

17. WJ, *Principles* 1:26, 121. Few of the secondary sources treat James's mechanistic starting point with any degree of seriousness. Wild, for example, discusses not mechanism but a conception of the self as a "living body"; while this may be the end toward which James was struggling, it was not where he began, and, above all, dismisses the problem of the self as James defined it. Jacques Barzun finds the argument of the *Principles* to be wholly antimechanistic, and ignores the opening chapters of James's text. See Wild, *Radical Empiricism*, Chap. 1; Barzun, *Stroll with William James*, p. 45.

18. WJ, *Principles* 1:1.

19. WJ, *Principles* 1:183.

20. WJ, *Principles* 1:181. For an analysis of James's views on the soul, see Theodore Flournoy, *The Philosophy of William James* (New York: Henry Holt, 1917), pp. 70ff. James's debt to Chauncy Wright on this issue is explained in a notice on Wright that James wrote for the *Nation* 21 (1875): 194.

21. WJ, *Principles* 1:2–3.

22. WJ, *Principles* 1:3, 5.

23. WJ, *Principles* 1:24–25.

24. WJ, *Principles* 1:26.

25. WJ, *Principles* 1:77.

26. WJ, *Principles* 1:140–41.

27. WJ, *Principles* 1:138.

28. WJ, *Principles* 1:132–33. James's point here was that scientific accuracy was compatible with subjective interests and should not be allowed to invoke authority before the fact on any given hypothesis. For a more extended discussion of these issues, see "Are We Automata?" *Mind* 4

(1879): 1–22); "Reflex Action and Theism," *Unitarian Review* 16 (1881): 389–416; "The Mood of Science and the Mood of faith," *Nation* 19 (1874): 437.

29. WJ, *Principles* 1:138.
30. WJ, *Principles* 1:224–25.
31. WJ, *Principles* 1:230.
32. WJ, *Principles* 1:239, 251, 254, 255. "What must be admitted is that the definite images of traditional psychology form but the very smallest part of our minds as they actually live. The traditional psychology talks like one who should say a river consists of nothing but pailsful, spoonsful, quartpotsful, barrelsful, and other moulded forms of water. Even were the pails and the pots all actually standing in the stream, still between them the free water would continue to flow. It is just this free water of consciousness that psychologists resolutely overlook" (*Principles* 1:255).
33. WJ, *Principles* 1:226, 284–85. For an early discussion of the role of interest and selection, see James's "Remarks on Spencer's Definition of Mind as Correspondence," in *Collected Essays and Reviews*, pp. 43–68.
34. WJ, *Principles* 1:226, 227.
35. WJ, *Principles* 1:288–89.
36. WJ, *Principles* 1:291. "We see then that we are dealing with a fluctuating material. The same object being sometimes treated as a part of me, at other times as simply mine, and then again as if I had nothing to do with it at all" (p. 291).
37. WJ, *Principles* 1:372, 310.
38. WJ, *Principles* 1:337, 297.
39. WJ, *Principles* 1:338.
40. WJ, *Principles* 1:365. For an analysis of the notion of self-identity, and its links to the more general understanding of consciousness, see Charlene Haddock Siegfried, *Chaos and Context* (Oberlin, OH: Oberlin Printing Co., 1978), chap. 1, pp. 10–39.
41. WJ, *Principles* 1:310–11.
42. WJ, *Principles* 1:453.
43. WJ, *Principles* 2:1.
44. WJ, *Principles* 2:7.
45. WJ, *Principles* 2:335, 547.
46. WJ, *Principles* 2:372, 330.
47. WJ, *Principles* 2:383.
48. WJ, *Principles* 2:333. See a letter by James to Alice James: "I have often thought that the best way to define a man's character would be to seek out the particular mental or moral attitude in which, when it came upon him, he felt himself most deeply and intensely active and alive. At such moments there is a voice inside which speaks and says: 'This is the real me.'

. . . Now as well as I can describe it, this characteristic attitude in me always involves an element of active tension, of holding my own, as it were, and trusting outward things to perform their part so as to make it a full harmony, but without any guaranty that they will. Make it a guaranty—and the attitude immediately becomes to my consciousness stagnant and stingless. Take away the guaranty, and I feel (provided I am *uberhaupt* in vigourous condition) a sort of deep enthusiastic bliss, of bitter willingness to do and suffer anything, which translates itself physically by a kind of stinging pain inside my breastbone (don't smile at this—it is to me an essential element of the whole thing) and which authenticates itself to me as the deepest principle of all active and theoretic determination which I possess" (*Letters* 1:199–200).

49. WJ, *Principles* 2:297, 321.

50. WJ, *Principles* 2:568, 559.

51. WJ, *Principles* 2:283, 290.

52. WJ, *Principles* 2:563–64. James's 1876 article on Charles Renouvier shows well his debt to Renouvier on the question of the will; see "Bain and Renouvier," in *Collected Essays and Reviews*, pp. 26–35.

53. Quoted in Perry, *Thought and Character* 2:90.

54. WJ, *Principles* 2:296–97, 311.

55. WJ, *Principles* 2:573.

56. WJ, *Principles* 2:564, 584.

57. WJ, "Rationality, Activity, and Faith," *Princeton Review* 2 (1882) : 58–86. The quotations were reprinted in the *Principles* 2:312–15.

58. WJ, *Principles* 2:547.

59. See WJ, *Principles* 1:453.

Chapter 3

1. William Dean Howells, "The New Historical Romance," *North American Review* 171 (1900): 936.

2. Jacob Riis, *How the Other Half Lives* (New York: Charles Scribner, 1890), p. 71. The phrase quoted is the title of chapter 23 of the book, in which Riis concludes his depiction of the urban scene of his day.

3. For an analysis and partial listing of these groups and titles, see T. J. J. Lears, *No Place of Grace* (New York: Pantheon Books, (1981), pp. 109–13. See also Van Wyck Brooks, *New England: Indian Summer, 1865–1915* (New York: E. P. Dutton and Co., 1940), p. 437, for a discussion of the rise of monarchist and royalist groups during this period.

4. Frederick Jackson Turner, "The Significance of the Frontier in American History," in *Proceedings of the Forty-First Annual Meeting of the*

State Historical Society of Wisconsin (Madison, 1884), p. 112. Turner presented his "frontier thesis" on July 12, 1893, at the World's Columbian Exposition in Chicago.

5. "New Thought," also a specific religious movement, is used here as a general name for a number of organizations (Mind Cure, Christian Science), and as a label for a general movement to merge traditional Christian beliefs and practices with the new sciences of the time. For a history of the movement, see Horatio Dresser, *A History of the New Thought Movement* (New York: Thomas Crowell, 1919). Stephen Gottschalk offers a summary of the links between the various religious groups that arose in the late nineteenth century; see *The Emergence of Christian Science in American Religious Life* (Berkeley: University of California Press, 1973), pp. 98–157.

6. Washington Gladden, *Ruling Ideas of the Present Age* (Boston: Houghton, Mifflin, 1895), p. 1. Gladden and other social gospel writers were, in respect to their notions of the power of ideas, within the general movement of New Thought. For an analysis of the relationship of New Thought to social reform movements, see Gottschalk, *Emergence of Christian Science*, pp. 249–96.

7. See, for example, the argument of Robert Handy in *A Christian America* (New York: Oxford University Press, 1971), pp. 117–54.

8. John DeForest, *A Lover's Revolt* (New York: Longmans, Green, 1898). DeForest had written primarily realistic works up to the publication of this novel.

9. Robert Underwood Johnson, "The Responsibility of the Magazine," *Independent* (1912): 1487–90. Quoted in Henry May, *The End of American Innocence* (New York: Alfred Knopf, 1959), p. 72.

10. Rudyard Kipling, *Something of Myself* (London: Macmillan, 1937), p. 118.

11. See Alan Trachtenberg, *The Incorporation of America* (New York: Hill and Wang, 1982), pp. 203ff.

12. For an analysis of this and the related "conspiratorial" views of history, see Richard Hofstadter, *Age of Reform* (New York: Vintage Press, 1955), pp. 60–81.

13. Turner, "The Frontier in American History," p. 112.

14. Henry Adams, *The Education of Henry Adams* (Boston: Houghton, Mifflin, 1918), p. 331.

15. George Herron, *The New Redemption* (New York: Thomas Y. Crowell, 1893), p. 121.

16. Sarah Whitman, *Letters of Sarah Wyman Whitman* (Cambridge, MA: Riverside Press, 1907), p. 188.

17. Lears discusses the emergence of a martial ideal in the late nine-

teenth century and its function as a form of therapy; see *No Place of Grace*, pp. 97–140.

18. Oliver Wendell Holmes, Jr., "Memorial Day," in *Speeches* (Boston: Little, Brown, 1896), p. 62.

19. Richard Hovey, *The Marriage of Guenevere* (New York: Duffield, 1891), act 4, sc. 1.

20. See, for example, the "Platform of the American Anti-Imperial League" (October 17, 1899), in *Great Issues in American History*, ed. Richard Hofstadter (New York: Vintage Press, 1958), pp. 202–4. As Hofstadter stated in his *Age of Reform* (p. 85), anti-imperialists were not against war as such: "What they chiefly objected to was institutional militarism rather than war itself, imperialism rather than jingoism. Under a patina of pacifist rhetoric they were profoundly nationalistic and bellicose."

21. Jacob Riis, *The Battle with the Slum* (New York: Macmillan, 1902), p. 7.

22. Social gospel writers, for example, combined Darwinian notions of survival and struggle with Christian doctrines of the providence of God and the coming of the kingdom of God. "Progress is not a smooth movement," wrote Gladden in *Ruling Ideas* (pp. 9–10); "it involves a struggle for existence and the survival of the fittest,—repudiation of the old, and painful assimilation of the new. The garment is rent; the wine-skin is burst."

23. Alexander Hamilton, "The Defects of the Articles of Confederation and the Need for a New Constitution," in *The Federalist Papers* (New York: Simon and Schuster, 1977), p. 1.

24. Oliver Wendell Holmes, Jr., "The Path of the Law," *Harvard Law Review* 10 (1897) : 457.

25. Quoted in Handy, *A Christian America*, p. 129.

26. Amory Bradford, "Socialism from the Socialistic Standpoint," quoted in Henry May, *Protestant Churches and Industrial America* (New York: Harper and Brothers, 1949), p. 223.

27. Howells, "The New Historical Romance," pp. 939–40.

28. Andrew Carnegie, "Wealth," *North American Review* 148 (1899): 656.

29. See Herron, *New Redemption*, p. 143.

30. See Albert Beveridge, "The March of the Flag," in *The Meaning of the Times* (Indianapolis: Bobbs-Merrill, 1908), pp. 47–57.

31. See, for example, Walter Rauschenbusch's use of knightly language in *For God and the People: Prayers of the Social Awakening* (Boston: Pilgrim Press, 1910), p. 23. Richard Hofstadter viewed this new mode of self-imagery as a successful but deceptive kind of self-manipulation: "In the old self-help system, faith led to character and character to successful manipulation of the world; in the new system, faith leads directly to a

capacity for self-manipulation, which is believed to be the key to health, wealth, popularity or peace of mind." *Anti-Intellectualism in American Life* (New York: Vintage Press, 1962), p. 266.

32. While the images of the knightly self were predominantly male, this was not always the case; Joan of Arc, for example, was considered an exemplary image of the authentic woman. See Mark Twain, *The Personal Recollections of Joan of Arc* (New York: Charles Scribner, 1896).

33. F. Marion Crawford, *Via Crucis, A Romance of the Second Crusade* (New York: Macmillan, 1899), p. 57.

34. See Lears, *No Place of Grace*, chap. 3, for a discussion of the distinctions between the knight and those other models of the self. For a different perspective which emphasizes the need for models of practical life instead of the soft, genius type, see Hofstadter, "The Practical Culture," in *Anti-Intellectualism*, pp. 233–98.

35. Gladden, *Ruling Ideas*, p. 258.

36. Josiah Strong, in his book *Our Country* (rev. ed 1891; rpt., Cambridge, MA: Harvard University Press, 1963), presented a sustained argument for the world dominance of the Anglo-Saxon race. See particularly his penultimate chapter, "The Anglo-Saxon and the World's Future."

37. See Albert Beveridge's "March of the Flag," in which almost all characteristics supporting his argument for imperial adventure are cast as American traits. As Sydney Mead put it in the *Lively Experiment* (New York: Harper and Row, 1963), p. 141: "Protestantism left the way open for the assimilation of any pattern of values that might seem good in the light of man's actual social experience . . . and has thus tended to become largely an emotional force in support of the reigning secular social ideals."

38. Walter Hines Page, "The War with Spain and After," *Atlantic Monthly* 82 (1898): 725.

39. Page, "The War with Spain," p. 726. Hines complained that his generation had not had opportunities for exercising their Anglo-Saxon identities: "But now a generation has come to manhood that has had no part in any great adventure. . . . The decline in the character of our public life has been a natural result of the lack of large constructive opportunities."

40. Edward Bellamy, *Looking Backward* (Boston: Ticknor, 1888).

41. Strong, *Our Country*, pp. 201, 213.

42. Beveridge, "The March of the Flag," p. 47.

43. Walt Whiman, "Democratic Vistas," in *Complete Poetry and Selected Prose of Walt Whitman* (Boston: Houghton, Mifflin, 1959), pp. 455–501.

44. See Lester Frank Ward, *Dynamic Sociology* (New York: D. Appleton, 1894).

45. Herron, *The New Redemption*, p. 29.

46. Dresser, *History of New Thought*, p. 161. See also Josiah Strong's argument that Christianity provided a "pure, spiritual religion," and hence would emerge as the dominant religious force in the world (*Our Country*, pp. 201–2).

47. See Rauschenbusch, *For God and the People*, p. 15.

48. Daniel Dorchester, *Christianity in the United States* (New York: Hunt and Eaton, 1895), p. 699.

49. Herron, *The New Redemption*, p. 14.

50. May, *Protestant Churches and Industrial America*, pt. 3, "Social Christianity."

51. Herron, *The New Redemption*, p. 29.

52. See Handy, *A Christian America*, chap. 5, "The Christian Conquest of the World."

53. Sydney Gulick, *The Growth of the Kingdom*, quoted in Handy, *A Christian America*, p. 123.

54. Rauschenbusch, *For God and the People*, p. 17.

55. Rauschenbusch, *For God and the People*, p. 17.

56. "The cannon has generally torn holes in the walls of barbarism and heathenism, through which the Gospel of Christ has had the most effective entrance. One reason why the Anglo-Saxon has carried the cross of Christ so high has been because the edge of his sword has been so keen." Ferdinand Inglehart, *New York Times* (March 28, 1898); quoted in Handy, *A Christian America*, p. 124.

57. Herron, *The New Redemption*, p. 62.

58. Quoted in William McLoughlin, *Revivals, Awakenings, and Reform* (Chicago: University of Chicago Press, 1969), p. 172.

59. Herron, *The New Redemption*, p. 18.

60. There were, of course, statements in abundance about the quality of life that would be found in this postrevolutionary state,—a world free of disease, poverty, and other social ills. And theocratic notions, in which the church would be "far more pervasive as an influence," were common. In all, however, the most that was said was that the new years "will not be less but more profoundly religious than the old." Ray Stannard Baker, *The Spiritual Unrest* (New York: Frederick Stokes, 1910), pp. 284–85.

61. See Mead, *The Lively Experiment*, p. 137.

Chapter 4

1. For a brief account of the occasion, and of James's role in it, see Gay Wilson Allen, *William James: A Biography* (New York: Viking, 1967),

pp. 387–88. James's address, "Robert Gould Shaw," can be found in *Memories and Studies* (New York: Longmans, Green, 1911), pp. 35–61.

2. William James to B. P. Blood, April 28, 1897, in *The Letters of William James*, ed. Henry James (Boston: Atlantic Monthly Press, 1920), 2:59.

3. WJ, *Letters*, 2:60.

4. WJ, *Letters*, 2:61. James had been a member of an expedition to South America led by Louis Agassiz. For a description of the expedition, see Allen, *William James*, pp. 110–16. James's brother Wilkinson had served with Colonel Shaw in the Fifty-fourth Regiment.

5. WJ, *Letters*, 2:60.

6. WJ, "Robert Gould Shaw," p. 42. Shaw had been commissioned to lead the Fifty-fourth Massachusetts Regiment, the first predominantly black regiment to be formed during the Civil War.

7. WJ, "Robert Shaw," pp. 39, 48, 42.

8. WJ, "Robert Shaw," pp. 43, 45, 58. Shaw had been, prior to his command of the Fifty-fourth Regiment, an officer in the prestigious Massachusetts Second.

9. WJ, "Robert Shaw," pp. 56, 57.

10. WJ, "Robert Shaw," p. 55.

11. The two major defining works of this period are James's 1896 Lowell lectures, *Exceptional Mental States*, reconstructed by Eugene Taylor (New York: Charles Scribner's Sons, 1983), and *The Will to Believe and Other Essays in Popular Philosophy* (New York: Longmans, Green, 1897). Most scholars have failed to treat James's work in the 1890s in terms of its rooting in the *Principles*, and have preferred to view it simply as the early formulation of later philosophical and religious themes. One of the few scholars to begin to make the linkage back to James's psychology is Henry Levinson, although, for the most part, he incorporates James's work in this period into the arguments of the *Varieties*. See Levinson's *Religious Investigations of William James* (Chapel Hill: University of North Carolina Press, 1981), pp. 71–94.

12. For James's position on white supremacy, see "A Strong Note of Warning Regarding the Lynching Epidemic," *Springfield Daily Republican* (July 23, 1903), p. 11. A general assessment of James's political concerns and positions can be found in R. B. Perry, *The Thought and Character of William James* (Boston: Little, Brown, 1935), 2:280–322.

13. WJ, "What Psychical Research Has Accomplished," in *Will to Believe*, p. 325.

14. WJ, "What Psychical Research Has Accomplished," p. 320. James's interest in and work for the Society for Psychical Research is examined in Perry, *Thought and Character*, 2:155–72.

15. WJ, *Exceptional Mental States*, p. 34.

16. WJ, *Exceptional Mental States*, p. 18.

17. For an examination of James's initial assessments of these wider frameworks, see R. B. Perry's chapter "The Right to Believe," in *In the Spirit of William James* (New Haven: Yale University Press, 1938), pp. 170–208. James's views were summarized in a letter to Henry Rankin: "We are thus made convincingly aware of the presence of a sphere of life larger and more powerful than our usual consciousness, with which the latter is nevertheless continuous. . . . Something, not our immediate self, does act on our life" (*Letters*, 2:150).

18. WJ, *Exceptional Mental States*, p. 15. See also Jacques Barzun, *A Stroll with William James* (New York: Harper and Row, 1983), pp. 142–80.

19. WJ, "Is Life Worth Living?" in *Will to Believe*, p. 41.

20. For the shift from a notion of "well-doing" to one of saving faith and "well-being," see Julius Seelye Bixler, *Religion in the Philosophy of William James* (Boston: Marshall Jones, 1926), pp. 122–32.

21. For a brief assessment of James's doctrine of the will to believe and of the "strenuous mood" of faith, see Levinson, *Religious Investigations*, pp. 51–56.

22. WJ, "Is Life Worth Living?" p. 62.

23. WJ, "Philosophical Conceptions and Practical Results," in *Collected Essays and Reviews*, ed. R. B. Perry (New York: Longmans, Green, 1920), p. 428.

24. WJ, "A Strong Note of Warning Regarding the Lynching Epidemic," p. 11.

25. WJ, "What Psychical Research Has Accomplished," pp. 326, 325. James was also battling those who would hold religion to be only a rational endeavor, something that omitted all of "the vitally important work" of religion. See Perry, *Thought and Character*, 2:322.

26. WJ, "What Psychical Research Has Accomplished," p. 325.

27. WJ, review of Hodgson's *Observations of Trance*, in *Collected Essays and Reviews*, p. 440.

28. WJ, "Philosophical Conceptions," pp. 428, 429.

29. James's notion of teleology remained, throughout the 1890s, couched in a medical and psychological definition of action as unobstructed and healthy on the whole. For a treatment of James's idea of responsible, healthy life, see John Wild, *The Radical Empiricism of William James* (Garden City, NY: Doubleday, 1969), pp. 265–92.

30. WJ, *Exceptional Mental States*, pp. 163–64.

31. WJ, *The Varieties of Religious Experience* (New York: Longmans, Green, 1902).

32. It is usual in treatments of James's Gifford lectures to interpret only

this stress against the materialists and to disregard his effort to move away from the romanticists. See Henry Levinson's treatment of the lectures in *Religious Investigations*; also Julius Bixler's interpretation in *Religion in William James*. Barzun gives a brief discussion of James's antiheroism in *Stroll with William James*, pp. 165–70, but does not comment on his religious investigations.

33. On the notion of a "science of religions," see Levinson, *Religious Investigations*, pp. 71–95; also Wild, *Radical Empiricism*, pp. 294–300. James gave a statement of his purpose in the lectures: "The problem I have set myself is a hard one: first, to defend (against all the prejudices of my class) experience against philosophy as being the real backbone of the world's religious life—I mean prayer, guidance, and all that sort of thing immediately and privately felt, as against the high and noble general views of our destiny and the world's meaning; and second, to make the hearer or reader believe, what I myself invincibly do believe, that, although all the special manifestations of religion may have been absurd (I mean its settled creeds and theories), yet the life of it as a whole is mankind's most important function. A task well-nigh impossible, I fear, and in which I shall fail; but to attempt it is my religious act" (*Letters*, 2:127).

34. For analyses of this sort, see particularly Elizabeth Flower and Murray Murphey, *A History of Philosophy in America*, vol. 2 (New York: G. P. Putnam's Sons, 1977; also Bruce Kuklick, *The Rise of American Philosophy* (New Haven: Yale University Press, 1977).

35. WJ, *Varieties*, p. 3.

36. WJ, *Varieties*, pp. 10, 12.

37. WJ, *Varieties*, pp. 3, 6–7. Edwin Starbuck, from whom James took many of his examples and citations, complained of James's extremism in a review for *Biblical World*. James replied at length that his examples, because they were extreme, cast more light on the phenomena of religious life than did the "tamer examples." For an account of the debate, see Perry, *Thought and Character*, 2:346.

38. WJ, *Varieties*, pp. 6, 24, 26.

39. WJ, *Varieties*, pp. 45, 47. In his notes for the lectures, James explained his position more fully: "The struggle seems to be that of a less articulate and more profound part of our nature to hold out, and keep itself standing, against the attempts of a more superficial and explicit or loquacious part, to suppress it. . . . I must frankly establish the breach between the life of articulate reason, and the push of the subconscious, the irrational instinctive part, which is more vital. . . . It is a question of life, of living in these gifts or not living." (quoted in Perry, *Thought and Character*, 2:327–28).

40. WJ, *Varieties*, p. 47.

41. WJ, *Varieties*, pp. 57, 58. Again, James founded his notion of religious reality on the general fact of consciousness as composed of a field plus an object plus an attitude and self-regard of the subject; see Theodore Flournoy, *The Philosophy of William James* (New York: Henry Holt, 1917), pp. 231–33.

42. WJ, *Varieties*, pp. 72, 64. For an analysis of James's understanding of religious facts, see Levinson, *Religious Investigations*, pp. 95–121.

43. WJ, *Varieties*, p. 141.

44. WJ, *Varieties*, pp. 80, 88. See also pp. 91–95 for a description of these popular forms of religiosity.

45. WJ, *Varieties*, pp. 90, 80.

46. WJ, *Varieties*, pp. 80, 93, 87. John Wild explains this idea in James's thought as a middle way between realism and idealism, and of healthy-mindedness as a partial view of things. See *Radical Empiricism*, pp. 301–13, for a discussion of healthy-mindedness and James's regard for it.

47. WJ, *Varieties*, p. 138.

48. WJ, *Varieties*, p. 142.

49. WJ, *Varieties*, pp. 137, 136, 139–40. As James explained in a letter to George Palmer: "A man whose egg at breakfast turns out always bad says to himself, 'Well, bad and good are not the same, anyhow.' That is just the trouble. Moreover, when you come down to the facts, what do your harmonious and integral ideal systems prove to be? in the concrete? Always things burst by the growing content of experience. Dramatic unities; laws of versification; ecclesiastical systems; scholastic doctrines. Bah!" (*Letters*, 2:213).

50. Most of James's description of the sick-soul need not be repeated here, as it remained the same as in his work of the 1890s. What he added, as I discuss, was an analysis of the nature of the sick-soul's crisis, and the conversion to a new state of life. For an argument supporting this view of conversion as the important addition to James's notion of the sick-soul, see Bixler, *Religion in William James*, pp. 191–92.

51. WJ, *Varieties*, p. 145.

52. WJ, *Varieties*, p. 144. James here added an exception to his general understanding that genius was not conditioned by a pathological temperament, although again, as I will show, the pathological extremities of the perception of evil in the sick-souled self were balanced by wider interests. The sick-soul was pathological but not out of touch, indeed, lived a more "real" life than the healthy-minded. For a treatment of these points, see Wild, *Radical Empiricism*, pp. 301–13.

53. WJ, *Varieties*, p. 153. Tolstoy, Luther, George Bunyan, and Saint Paul stood for James as representatives of the sick-souled type, both in their vision of life and in their recovery from the effects of that vision.

54. WJ, *Varieties*, pp. 166, 171. The notion of a divided will, and its cure through conversion, was explained by James in a letter to Henry Rankin: "It is a case of the conflict of two self-systems in a personality up to that time heterogeneously divided, but in which, after the conversion-crisis, the higher loves and powers come definitively to gain the upper hand and expel the forces which up to that time had kept them down in the position of mere grumblers and protesters and agents of remorse and discontent. This broader view will cover an enormous number of cases psychologically, and leaves all the religious importance to the result which it has on any other theory" (*Letters*, 2:57).

55. WJ, *Varieties*, pp. 163, 161. For the account of James's melancholic crisis, see pp. 160–61.

56. WJ, *Varieties*, p. 162. Levinson notes the link between James's psychological notions of regeneration and the more strictly religious notion of salvation; see *Religious Investigations*, pp. 114–21.

57. WJ, *Varieties*, p. 212. For an analysis of this shift from the doctrine of the will to believe, and more generally from the construction of belief in the *Principles*, see Bixler, *Religion in William James*, pp. 122ff.

58. WJ, *Varieties*, p. 157.

59. WJ, *Varieties*, p. 187.

60. See WJ, *Varieties*, p. 194. James did, of course, accept a common sense notion of integration rather than a change and instilling of a wholly new nature. Stated very generally, conversion, redemption, and so on were not allowed to override the "lowly origins" of religiosity that James had set forth in his initial lectures.

61. WJ, *Varieties*, p. 196.

62. WJ, *Varieties*, p. 211; see also pp. 205ff.

63. For an examination of the understanding of "consent" in James's religious thought, see Richard Comstock, "William James and the Logic of Religious Belief," *Journal of Religion* 47 (1967): 196; also Paul Van Buren, "William James and Metaphysical Risk," in *Philosophy and the Future*, ed. Michael Novak (New York: Scribner's Sons, 1968), pp. 87–106.

64. WJ, *Varieties*, p. 210.

65. See WJ, *Varieties*, p. 207. James's imprecision here was characteristic of his view that scientific hypotheses are responses from as well as predispositions toward facts. For a general discussion of the relationship between James's religious views and his scientific methods, see Robert Vanden Burgt, *The Religious Philosophy of William James* (Chicago: Nelson Hall, 1981), pp. 35–43.

66. See WJ, *Varieties*, pp. 233, 234. Levinson discusses James's efforts to overcome the rift between theologians and scientists with his idea of the ultramarginal and subliminal; see *Religious Investigations*, pp. 113–18.

67. The specifics about divinity were always no more than modes of conjecture, or at most of personal conviction; the unseen was real and definite, but its definitions were always of something unseen. James would deal with this matter more completely in his lecture "Mysticism," where he concluded that the naming of divinity was no more than a personal statement.

68. See WJ, *Varieties*, pp. 259–325.

69. WJ, *Varieties*, pp. 331, 337, 339–40.

70. WJ, *Varieties*, pp. 343, 354.

71. See WJ, *Varieties*, p. 355. Levinson sees the value of saintliness for James as a matter of simplification, and as a way of breaking a consumerist pattern of living in which "having" rather than "being" was held as ultimate. See *Religious Investigations*, pp. 118–21. This was certainly a part of James's understanding of the saintly life; the central point, however, was not simplification but refusal, a political more than a private way of life.

72. WJ, *Varieties*, pp. 355, 357, 360.

73. WJ, *Varieties*, p. 362.

74. WJ, *Varieties*, pp. 371, 372. To be sure, James caricatured the Nietzschean model of the self, neglecting Nietzsche's refusal of popular, typical models of action. James was on the mark, however, in his understanding that Nietzsche presented the strongest case for a life lived according to principles of self-assertion.

75. WJ, *Varieties*, pp. 372, 375. James's argument from ideals was intended more as an aside than as a substantive point, proof of the value of his model as a soul-sustaining myth.

76. WJ, *Varieties*, pp. 374–75.

77. WJ, *Varieties*, p. 376.

78. WJ, *Varieties*, pp. 377, 369.

79. WJ, *Varieties*, p. 356. See "Robert Shaw," p. 59.

Chapter 5

1. See WJ, *The Varieties of Religious Experience* (New York: Longmans, Green, 1902), lectures 16–20.

2. WJ, *Varieties*, p. 527.

3. WJ, *Varieties*, p. 398.

4. WJ, *Varieties*, p. 508. This remained James's working definition of religion throughout the rest of his writings; see, for example, his concluding lecture in *A Pluralistic Universe* (Cambridge, MA: Harvard University Press, 1977), p. 139.

5. See WJ, *Varieties*, pp. 526-27. Also, see Henry Levinson's chapter on the Gifford lectures for an analysis of the importance of the "chance for salvation" in James's religious thought, in *The Religious Investigations of William James* (Chapel Hill: University of North Carolina Press, 1981), pp. 71-167.

6. WJ, *The Letters of William James*, ed. Henry James (Boston: Atlantic Monthly Press, 1920), 2:205.

7. WJ, *Varieties*, p. 523.

8. WJ, *Essays in Radical Empiricism*, ed. R. B. Perry (New York: Longmans, Green, 1912), p. 39.

9. The articles were written in the years 1904-5. James collected reprints of the articles toward the end of his career and arranged them for publication as a book.

10. WJ, *Essays*, pp. 36, 33.

11. WJ, *Essays*, pp. 3-4. For an overall analysis of James's radical empiricism, see John Wild, *The Radical Empiricism of William James* (Garden City, NY: Doubleday, 1969), pp. 359-88; also Charlene Haddock Siegfried, *Chaos and Context* (Oberlin, OH: Oberlin Printing Co., 1978). R. B. Perry gives a summary and extension of James's empiricism in "The Metaphysics of Experience," in *In the Spirit of William James* (New Haven: Yale University Press, 1938), pp. 75-123.

12. WJ, *Essays*, p. 23.

13. James returned here to the "neutral" starting point of his investigation of belief in the *Principles*. For an examination of the links between the *Principles* and the *Essays*, see Siegfried's opening chapter in *Chaos and Context*, pp. 10-29; also Elizabeth Flower and Murray Murphey, *A History of Philosophy in America* (New York: G. P. Putnam's Sons, 1977), 2:662-73.

14. WJ, *Essays*, pp. 9-10.

15. WJ, *Essays*, p. 272.

16. WJ, *The Principles of Psychology* (New York: Henry Holt, 1890), 1:224-90.

17. James arranged these conjunctive relations in a hierarchy of increasing intimacy: "With, near, next, like, from, towards, against, for, through, my—these words designate types of conjunctive relation arranged in a roughly ascending order of intimacy and inclusiveness" (*Essays*, p. 45).

18. WJ, *Essays*, pp. 42, 86-87.

19. WJ, *Essays*, pp. 77, 76. See also the later article in the *Essays* entitled "Is Radical Empiricism Solipsistic?" pp. 234-40.

20. WJ, *Essays*, p. 169.

21. WJ, *Essays*, p. 87.

22. See "The Thing and Its Relations," and "How Two Minds Can Know One Thing," in *Essays*, pp. 92–136.

23. WJ, *Essays*, p. 95. For a discussion of James's concatenated reality and its leadings into panpsychism, see Peter Marcus Ford, *William James' Philosophy* (Amherst: University of Massachusetts Press, 1982), pp. 75–84.

24. WJ, *Essays*, p. 140. Having given an intimate world, James had now to return to the question that had been central in his earlier works, the question of productive purpose. James would work this issue through the rest of his writings; although he provided an adequate resolution in the *Essays*, it was not until the Hibbert lectures (*A Pluralistic Universe*) that he gave a complete response.

25. WJ, "The Place of Affectional Facts in a World of Pure Experience," in *Essays*, pp. 137–54 passim. John McDermott offers an analysis of affectional facts in his "radically empirical aesthetic," in "To Be Human Is to Humanize," in *Philosophy and the Future*, ed. Michael Novak (New York: Charles Scribner's Sons, 1968), pp. 21–59.

26. WJ, *Essays*, pp. 138, 152.

27. WJ, *Essays*, p. 138. Affectional facts, as James explained, traditionally were considered to be derivable only from consciousness, and stood as a refutation of an empiricist model.

28. WJ, *Essays*, p. 142; see also *Principles*, vol. 2, chap. 25.

29. WJ, *Essays*, p. 146.

30. WJ, "The Experience of Activity," address delivered in Philadelphia, December 1904. See *Essays*, pp. 155–89.

31. WJ, *Essays*, pp. 161, 164, 184. Again, James was updating his formulations in the *Principles*, moving from a gallery (needing a curator) to a landscape with its own organic connections. See Wild's analysis of affections in "World Facts," in *Radical Empiricism*, pp. 378–81, for a treatment of this move from the psychology.

32. WJ, *Essays*, p. 174. James would return to this notion of "activity-situations" in his last, unfinished work, *Some Problems of Philosophy* (New York: Longmans, Green, 1911), where he would link up the notion of activity as work with that of creativity and the new.

33. WJ, *Essays*, p. 166.

34. WJ, *Essays*, p. 172. Again, see also James's *Some Problems*, particularly the chapter on causation, pp. 166–219.

35. WJ, *Essays*, p. 182.

36. WJ, *Essays*, p. 185.

37. WJ, *Essays*, p. 186. For a discussion of James's position here, and his argument against the rationalists, see Siegfried, *Chaos and Context*, pp. 71–88.

38. WJ, *Essays*, p. 186.

39. WJ, *Essays*, pp. 180, 186–87.

40. WJ, *Pragmatism* (New York: Longmans, Green, 1907), p. 108. For an overview of James's pragmatism, see H. S. Thayer, *Meaning and Action: A Study of American Pragmatism* (Indianapolis: Bobbs-Merrill, 1973), esp. pp. 178–87. Phillip Wiener provides an assessment of the scientific and philosophical background behind James's pragmatism in *Evolution and the Founders of Pragmatism* (Cambridge, MA: Harvard University Press, 1947), pp. 97–128.

41. WJ, *Pragmatism*, p. 122. Again, the major argument of *Pragmatism* was to define the kinds of possibility afoot in the world; having defined the world of experience as a world of possibility, now the questions of direction, purpose, and criteria for evaluating experience needed to be discussed.

42. WJ, *Pragmatism*, p. 69. For an overview of James's pragmatism and its relationship to the problems of religious experience and truth, *Religious Investigations*, pp. 209–39.

43. WJ, *Pragmatism*, p. 45. See also James's essay "The Pragmatic Account of Truth and Its Misunderstanders," in *The Meaning of Truth* (New York: Longmans, Green, 1909), where James distinguished his idea of truth as a judgment on the work of a belief from the criticism that its only point was to gain some "practical advantage."

44. WJ, *Pragmatism*, passim. See also James's arguments against "logomachy" in "The Thing and Its Relations," in *Essays*, pp. 100–106.

45. Quoted in WJ, *Essays*, p. 238.

46. See the fifth lecture in *Pragmatism*, where James discussed pragmatism as a common sense formulation and vision, and the seventh lecture, where he linked his pragmatism to humanism. As James explained it in an interview with the *New York Times*, pragmatism had as its motive practical change: "In point of fact, the use of most of our thinking is to help us to change the world. . . . The pragmatist writers have shown that what we here call theoretic truth will be irrelevant unless it fits the purpose at hand." Quoted in R. B. Perry, *The Thought and Character of William James* (Boston: Little, Brown, 1935), 2:479.

47. WJ, *Pragmatism*, p. 22.

48. WJ, *Pragmatism*, p. 22.

49. WJ, *Pragmatism*, p. 218.

50. WJ, *Pragmatism*, pp. 139, 144.

51. WJ, *Pragmatism*, pp. 240–41.

52. WJ, *Pragmatism*, p. 259.

53. For James's understanding of the relationship between pragmatism and religion, and for a comparison of James and other pragmatists on the issue of religion, see John Smith, *Purpose and Thought: The Meaning of*

Pragmatism (New Haven: Yale University Press, 1978); pp. 159–94. In James's work the criteria for evaluating religious truths were, again, the work they did in practice: "On pragmatic principles we cannot reject any hypothesis if consequences useful to life flow from it. Universal conceptions, as things to take account of, may be real for pragmatism as particular sensations are. They have, indeed, no meaning and no reality if they have no use. But if they have any use they have that amount of meaning" *Purpose and Thought* (p. 273)

54. WJ, *Pragmatism*, pp. 280–82.

55. WJ, *Pragmatism*, pp. 286, 290, 288, 298.

56. WJ, *Pragmatism*, pp. 296–98. James returned here to his idea, developed in the *Varieties*, of conversion: to be converted was not, like the once-born life, to have everything taken up into an all-embracing unity; conversion was a loss and a gain, a matter of empirical overcoming. In his Hibbert lectures James would expand this point, seeing all movement in experience based on this conversion model.

57. WJ, *Pragmatism*, p. 290.

58. WJ, *Pluralistic Universe*, pp. 26–27. In these lectures James came as close as he ever did to a complete rejection of monistic idealism, allowing it only as a possible hypothesis that could not be held dogmatically. James's argument, however, went much further in its refutation than James himself would go.

59. WJ, *Pluralistic Universe*, p. 17.

60. WJ, *Pluralistic Universe*, p. 23.

61. WJ, *Pluralistic Universe*, p. 35.

62. WJ, *Pluralistic Universe*, p. 32.

63. WJ, *Pluralistic Universe*, p. 41.

64. WJ, *Pluralistic Universe*, p. 45. For an earlier treatment of Hegel, see James's essay "On Some Hegelisms," in *The Will to Believe and Other Essays in Popular Philosophy* (New York: Longmans, Green, 1897), pp. 263–98.

65. WJ, *Pluralistic Universe*, p. 45.

66. WJ, *Pluralistic Universe*, p. 52.

67. WJ, *Pluralistic Universe*, p. 52.

68. WJ, *Pluralistic Universe*, p. 61.

69. WJ, *Pluralistic Universe*, p. 62.

70. WJ, *Pluralistic Universe*, p. 99.

71. WJ, *Pluralistic Universe*, pp. 127, 121. More will be said about this crisis in the concluding chapter of this book; suffice it to say here that, again, the crisis fit the pattern of James's conversion model, where old ways could not be taken up but had to be overcome. For an account of James's crisis, see Perry, *Thought and Character*, 2:588–90. James kept a journal of

sorts during the years 1905-8, in which he discussed his turn of mind; selections from the journal appear in *Thought and Character*, vol. 2, app. 10, pp. 750-65.

72. WJ, *Pluralistic Universe*, pp. 125, 131. As James recognized, his empiricism and pragmatism were now linked and could not be left as two separate visions.

73. WJ, *Pluralistic Universe*, p. 132. For a discussion of James's relationship with Fechner, see chap. 87 in Perry, *Thought and Character*, pp. 618-36.

74. WJ, *Pluralistic Universe*, pp. 70, 78, 97.

75. WJ, *Pluralistic Universe*, pp. 106, 120.

76. WJ, *Pluralistic Universe*, p. 149. Toward the close of his career, James wrote several articles paying his debt of gratitude to those whom he saw as on the fringe of the philosophical circle. See, for example, James's last published article, on B. P. Blood, "A Pluralistic Mystic," in *Memories and Studies* (New York: Longmans, Green, 1911), pp. 369-411.

77. See James's chapter on mysticism in *Varieties*, pp. 379-429.

78. WJ, *Pluralistic Universe*, p. 128.

79. WJ, *Pluralistic Universe*, p. 138.

80. WJ, *Pluralistic Universe*, p. 145.

81. WJ, *Pluralistic Universe*, p. 30.

82. WJ, *Pluralistic Universe*, p. 54.

83. WJ, *Pluralistic Universe*, pp. 148-49.

Conclusion

1. WJ, *Some Problems of Philosophy, A Beginning of an Introduction to Philosophy* (New York: Longmans, Green, 1911). The published volume was prepared by Horace Kallen after James's death.

2. Johann Wolfgang von Goethe, *Works* (Stuttgart: 1827), 53:1, 19.

3. WJ, *Some Problems*, p. 140.

4. WJ, *Some Problems*, p. 189.

5. WJ, *Some Problems*, p. 139.

6. WJ, *Some Problems*, p. 225.

7. See James's chapter "Novelty and Causation—The Perceptual View," in *Some Problems*, pp. 208-19.

8. Compare James's vision to the "Adamic" vision of his father, Henry James, Sr.; for an analysis of James's Adamic vision, see R. W. B. Lewis, "The Fortunate Fall, " in *The American Adam* (Chicago: University of Chicago Press, 1955).

9. WJ, *Some Problems*, p. 142.

10. George Santayana, *The Genteel Tradition*, ed. Douglas Wilson (Cambridge, MA: Harvard University Press, 1967), p. 58.

11. Quoted by Santayana in *Genteel Tradition*, p. 58.

12. WJ, "Address at the Emerson Centenary in Concord," in *Memories and Studies* (New York: Longmans, Green, 1911), p. 19.

13. See "Conclusion" to the *Varieties of Religious Experience* (New York: Longmans, Green, 1902), where James gave his summary definition of religion and the religious life as consisting of two parts: "1. An uneasiness; and 2. Its solution. 1. The uneasiness, reduced to its simplest terms, is a sense that there is something wrong about us as we naturally stand. 2. The solution is a sense that we are saved from the wrongness" (p. 508).

14. See WJ, *Some Problems*, p. 224, where James defined the faith ladder and its various grades.

15. WJ, *Principles of Psychology* (New York: Henry Holt, 1890), 1:316.

16. The general point here is that James understood the exceptional not as unique but as representative and original.

17. For a discussion of James's position on morality and religion, see John Smith, *Purpose and Thought: The Meaning of Pragmatism* (New Haven: Yale University Press, 1978), pp. 159–61.

18. WJ, *Pragmatism* (New York: Longmans, Green, 1907), p. 4.

19. As James put it in his final "Introduction": "The original in which fact comes is the perceptual *durcheinander*, holding terms as well as relations in solution. Our reflective mind abstracts divers aspects in the muchness, as a man by looking through a tube may limit his attention to one part after another of a landscape. But abstraction is not insulation; and it no more breaks reality than the tube breaks the landscape" (*Some Problems*, p. 199).

20. WJ, *The Letters of William James* (Boston: Atlantic Monthly Press, 1920), 2:156.

21. WJ, "A Pluralistic Mystic," in *Memories and Studies*, p. 409.

22. "I fully believe that such an empiricism is a more natural ally than dialectics ever were, or can be, of the religious life. It is true that superstitions and wild-growing overbeliefs of all sorts will undoubtedly begin to abound. . . . But ought one seriously to allow such a timid consideration as that to deter one from following the evident path of greatest religious promise? Since when, in this mixed world, was any good thing given us in purest outline and isolation?" *A Pluralistic Universe* (Cambridge, MA: Harvard University Press, 1977), p. 142.

23. A partial exception to this tendency needs to be mentioned here, which has to do with the anti-German sentiment following the First World War. As philosophical idealism was popularly linked to German philosophy, it suffered a decline in the postwar years. For a discussion of this

decline, see Bruce Kuklick's chapter "Philosophers at War," in *The Rise of American Philosophy* (New Haven: Yale University Press, 1977), pp. 435–47. For a general discussion of the fate of James's work, see R. W. Sleeper, "Pragmatism, Religion and Experienceable Difference," in *Philosophy and the Future*, ed. Michael Novak (New York: Charles Scribner's Sons, 1968), pp. 271–73.

24. See, for example, Julius Bixler's concluding chapter in *Religion in the Philosophy of William James* (Boston: Marshall Jones, 1926).

25. For a summary (and extension) of this tradition about James, see Jacques Barzun, "The Genius," in *A Stroll with William James* (New York: Harper and Row, 1983), pp. 262–302.

26. The phrase is from George Santayana, *The Genteel Tradition*, p. 56.

27. For a discussion of this tendency, see the introduction to Richard Rorty, *The Consequences of Pragmatism* (Minneapolis: University of Minnesota Press, 1982).

28. Bixler, *Religion in the Philosophy of William James.*

29. Richard Rorty provides a brief summary of the history of pragmatism in "Pragmatism Without Method," in *Objectivity, Relativism, and Truth* (Cambridge: Cambridge University Press, 1991), pp. 63ff.

30. For a discussion of these basic tenets of pragmatism, see Henry Levinson, "Pragmatic Naturalism and the Spiritual Life," *Raritan* 10, (Fall 1990): 70–86.

31. Levinson, "Pragmatic Naturalism and the Spiritual Life," p. 70.

32. See Richard Rorty, *Contingency, Irony, and Solidarity* (Cambridge: Cambridge University Press, 1989), esp. chap. 1.

33. See Barzun, *A Stroll with William James*, pp. 301–2, where the author identifies the center of James's thought as a matter of complexity and "thickness" in life.

34. Rorty, *Contingency, Irony, and Solidarity*, p. 45.

35. Rorty, *Contingency, Irony, and Solidarity*, p. 45.

36. For a valorization of this goal, see Rorty's chapter on the contingency of the self, chapter 2 in *Contingency, Irony, and Solidarity*.

Index

Abbott, Lyman, 75–76
Absolutism, 122, 123–24
Action, 131
Activity, 111–12
"Activity situations," 131
Affectional experiences, 110–11
Agassiz, Louis, 34
American Nervousness: Its Causes and Consequences (Beard), 147*n*.1
American Psychological Association, 111
Anglo-Saxonism, 69–70, 74
Anti-Christ, The (Nietzsche), quotation from, 59
APA. *See* American Psychological Association
Appreciations. *See* Affectional experiences
Asceticism, 99, 100
Ashmore, William, 65
Associationist psychology, 34, 39–40
Automatism, 41–42

"Bare activity," 111
Barrie, James M., 62
Barzun, Jacques, 152*n*.14
Battle with the Slum (Riis), 64
Beard, George Miller, 147*n*.1
Beecher, Henry Ward, 19
Belief, 50–52, 84, 90–91, 97
Bellamy, Edward, 70
Bergson, Henri, 125
Beveridge, Albert, 70
Bible, 30–31

Blood, Benjamin Paul, 77, 137
Boston Metaphysical Club, 20
Bowne, Borden, 31, 32
Bradford, Amory, 66
Briggs, Charles, 27
Brooks, Phillips, 26
Bunyan, John, 32
Bushnell, Horace, 21

Calvinist theology, 28–29
Carnegie, Andrew, 66–67
Charity, 99–100
Christian Science, 155*n*.5
"City Without a Church, The" (Drummond), 26
Civil War, American, 5, 6, 9
    and the corporate order, 61
    cultural collapse following, 18–25
    reinterpretation of, 63
Columbian Exposition of 1893 (Chicago), 62
Conjunctive relations, 108
Consciousness, 81, 106–7
    stream image of, 43–45, 46
    train image of, 44
    transforming powers of, 50–51
Contingency, 10, 11, 13
Conversion, 52–54, 95–98

Darwinist psychology, 34, 41–42
DeForest, John, 61
DeKoven, James, 27
Democracy as theocracy, 74–75, 158*n*.60

173

174

Index

176 Index

Pluralism, 85–86, 114, 120–21, 124
monism v., 116–17, 124
Pluralistic Universe, A (W. James), 8,
113, 114, 120
Portrait of a Lady (W. James),
quotation from, 33–34
Pragma, 115
Pragmatism, 85–86, 113–16
"melioristic" doctrine in, 118–19
and rationalism, 117–18
and truth, 117
William James and tradition of,
140–42
"Pragmatism and Humanism"
(W. James), 117–18
"Pragmatism and Religion"
(W. James), 118
Pragmatism (W. James), 8, 113–14,
123
Principles of Psychology, The
(W. James), 8, 12, 80, 97, 110,
112, 146n.10
baby before candleflame image in,
40–42
belief in, 50–52, 83–84
consciousness described in, 43–45,
46–47
emotions theory in, 110–11
and *Essays in Radical Experience*,
107–8, 119–20
human, popular tone of, 33–36
John Dewey on, 35
limitations of, 54–56
organization of, 37–38, 39, 40, 48,
151n.10
personality described in, 45
quotation from, 17
religion treated in, 52–54, 83–85, 134
and republican ideal, 55
reviews and criticism of, 34–35
self depicted in, 40–43, 45–56, 104–5,
119
and *Varieties of Religious
Experience*, 87, 89
Protestantism
denominationalism of, 27
response to post–Civil War cultural
crisis, 25–27
"Psychologist's fallacy," 34
Psychology, portraiture used in, 38.
See also Associationist

psychology; Darwinist psychology;
Experimentalist psychology;
Spiritualist psychology
"Psychology as So-Called Natural
Science" (Ladd), 35

Radical empiricism, 105–6, 108, 120–22
Rationalism, 115–16, 117
"Rationality, Activity, and Faith"
(W. James), 53
Rauschenbusch, Walter, 75
Realists, 13–14
Religion. *See also under* Historical
romanticism
denominationalism of, 27
and experience, 138
and post–Civil War cultural crisis,
25–27, 31–32
private and institutional in America,
29–31
Religious experience, 88
"Religious Situation, The" (Smith), 32
Richardson, James, 25
Riis, Jacob, 59–60, 64
Rilke, Rainer Maria, 129
Romanticism. *See* Historical
romanticism
Ruling Ideas of the Present Age
(Gladden), 60–61

Saint-Gaudens, Augustus, 79
Saintly self, 93, 98–102, 164n.71
Salvation, 118–19, 127, 132, 136–37
Santayana, George, 36, 132
Security. *See under* Freedom
Self, 6, 7, 8, 11, 37. *See also* Historical
romanticism; Knighthood; Saintly
self; Sick-souled self; Wider self
after Civil War, 20, 22
associationist model of, 39–40
and "divine," 85
empirical, 45–46
and God, 28, 104–5
objective, 46
in *Principles of Psychology*, 41
in a relational world, 13–14
and religious belief, 90–91, 94
and religious conversion, 95–98
as religious militant, 74
spiritual, 39
theater of, 47–48, 53